MONEY PSYCHOLOGY

Money psychology is a multifaceted and intricate field that delves into the intricate relationship between individuals and their finances. It explores the complex interplay of emotions, behaviors, and cognitive processes that shape our attitudes towards money, influencing the way we earn, spend, save, and invest. Understanding money psychology is not merely an academic pursuit; it holds profound implications for personal financial well-being, economic stability, and societal dynamics.

At its core, money psychology encompasses the various psychological factors that impact our financial decision-making. From the early stages of childhood development to adulthood, individuals form beliefs, habits, and attitudes towards money that are deeply rooted in their psyche. These psychological imprints influence financial behaviors throughout one's life, often operating at a subconscious level.

One of the fundamental aspects of money psychology is the emotional connection people have with money. Emotions such as fear, greed, anxiety, and contentment play a pivotal role in shaping financial decisions. Understanding the emotional dimensions of money is crucial, as it sheds light on why individuals may make seemingly irrational financial choices. For some, money represents security and stability, while for others, it may symbolize power, status, or even self-worth.

1

The study of money psychology also delves into the cognitive processes that underlie financial decision-making. Behavioral economics, a field that combines insights from psychology and economics, has revealed the presence of cognitive biases that impact how individuals assess risks, make investment decisions, and plan for the future. Anchoring, loss aversion, and confirmation bias are just a few examples of cognitive biases that can lead to suboptimal financial choices.

Closely related to cognitive processes is the concept of financial literacy. Money psychology recognizes that individuals vary in their levels of financial knowledge and understanding. A lack of financial literacy can contribute to poor financial decision-making, reinforcing the importance of education and awareness in navigating the complexities of personal finance. Efforts to enhance financial literacy aim to empower individuals to make informed choices and build a solid foundation for their financial well-being.

Moreover, societal and cultural factors play a significant role in shaping money psychology. Cultural norms, family upbringing, and societal expectations influence the way individuals perceive money and engage with it. The concept of "keeping up with the Joneses" reflects the social aspect of money, where individuals compare themselves to others and make financial decisions based on social expectations rather than personal values.

The advent of technology has also introduced new dimensions to money psychology. The rise of digital currencies, online banking, and financial apps has transformed the way people interact with money. The immediacy and accessibility of financial information can impact decision-making processes, leading to both positive and negative outcomes.

Additionally, the broader economic context and global financial landscapes contribute to money psychology. Economic downturns, market volatility, and job insecurity can evoke strong emotional responses and influence financial behaviors on a macro scale. Understanding how individuals and societies react to economic challenges is crucial for policymakers, financial institutions, and individuals seeking to navigate turbulent financial climates.

Money psychology extends beyond individual behavior to encompass the dynamics of financial relationships. Couples, families, and business partners navigate complex financial landscapes that require effective communication, shared values, and collaborative decision-making. The intersection of interpersonal relationships and money introduces a layer of complexity that requires a nuanced understanding of both psychological and financial dynamics.

In conclusion, the study of money psychology is a fascinating exploration of the intricate relationship between the human mind and financial decision-making. From the emotional dimensions of money to cognitive biases, cultural influences, and the impact of technology, money psychology offers a comprehensive lens through which to understand the complexities of personal finance. As individuals, societies, and economies continue to evolve, a deeper understanding of money psychology becomes increasingly vital for fostering financial well-being and resilience in an ever-changing world.

Money and Emotions

The emotional relationship with money is a deeply ingrained aspect of human behavior that significantly influences financial decisions. From the joy of a windfall to the anxiety of debt, emotions play a central role in shaping how individuals perceive, approach, and manage their finances. This intricate interplay between emotions and money is a dynamic and complex phenomenon that spans across various aspects of personal finance.

At its core, the emotional relationship with money is rooted in the way individuals attach emotions to financial experiences. Positive emotions, such as happiness, satisfaction, and a sense of accomplishment, often accompany financial successes, such as receiving a raise, achieving a savings goal, or making a profitable investment. On the flip side, negative emotions, such as stress, fear, and guilt, may arise from financial setbacks, such as job loss, debt accumulation, or unexpected expenses.

The impact of emotions on financial decisions is evident in everyday choices related to spending, saving, and investing. Understanding this impact requires an exploration of the key emotional drivers that influence financial behavior.

Fear and anxiety are powerful emotions that can significantly affect financial decision-making. The fear of financial instability or economic downturns may lead individuals to adopt conservative financial strategies, such as hoarding cash or avoiding investments. Anxiety about debt can result in individuals making hasty decisions to reduce debt, sometimes at the expense of long-term financial goals. Recognizing and managing fear and anxiety are crucial for making rational and informed financial decisions.

On the opposite end of the spectrum, greed and overconfidence can drive individuals to take excessive risks in the pursuit of financial gains. Overestimating one's ability to predict market movements or underestimating the potential downsides of an investment can lead to imprudent financial decisions. Balancing ambition with a realistic assessment of risks is essential for avoiding the pitfalls associated with greed and overconfidence.

Financial windfalls or successes can trigger feelings of happiness and contentment. However, if not managed carefully, these positive emotions can lead to lifestyle inflation – an increase in spending to match the newfound income or wealth. Understanding the potential impact of happiness on spending habits is crucial for maintaining financial stability and avoiding the pitfalls of unsustainable lifestyle choices.

Regret about past financial decisions, whether it's a missed investment opportunity or a major financial mistake, can linger and influence future choices. Individuals may become overly cautious or hesitant to take risks due to the fear of repeating past errors. Overcoming regret involves learning from mistakes, forgiving oneself, and adopting a forward-looking approach to financial decision-making.

The social aspect of money introduces emotions tied to social comparison and peer pressure. Individuals may feel compelled to match the financial achievements of their peers, leading to lifestyle choices and spending patterns that are not aligned with their values or financial goals. Recognizing the impact of social influences and establishing a personal financial identity are essential for making authentic and intentional financial decisions.

Stressful situations, whether related to work, relationships, or health, can trigger impulsive spending as a coping mechanism. Retail therapy or indulgent purchases may provide temporary relief from stress but can contribute to long-term financial challenges. Developing healthy coping mechanisms and addressing the root causes of stress are crucial for mitigating the impact of stress on financial decisions.

Understanding the emotional drivers of financial decisions is the first step toward developing emotional intelligence in the realm of personal finance. Emotional intelligence involves recognizing and managing one's own emotions and understanding how emotions impact others. In the context of money, emotional intelligence empowers individuals to make rational, informed, and goal-aligned financial decisions.

The impact of emotions on financial decisions is further compounded by cognitive biases – systematic patterns of deviation from norm or rationality in judgment. Behavioral economics, a field that combines insights from psychology and economics, has identified various cognitive biases that influence financial decision-making. These biases often work in tandem with emotions, shaping the way individuals process information and make choices.

Loss aversion is a cognitive bias where individuals place more emphasis on avoiding losses than on acquiring equivalent gains. This bias can lead to risk aversion and a reluctance to make necessary but potentially challenging financial decisions. Overcoming loss aversion involves reframing losses as opportunities for growth and recognizing the importance of balanced risk-taking.

Anchoring is the tendency to rely too heavily on the first piece of information encountered when making decisions. In the context of money, individuals may anchor their financial decisions based on initial reference points, such as the purchase price of an asset or the amount of debt owed. Being aware of anchoring biases allows individuals to critically evaluate financial information and avoid making decisions solely based on arbitrary reference points.

Confirmation bias is the inclination to interpret new evidence as confirmation of one's existing beliefs or theories. In the realm of money, individuals may seek information that aligns with their preconceived notions about investments, spending habits, or financial goals. Mitigating confirmation bias involves actively seeking diverse perspectives and challenging one's own assumptions.

The availability heuristic is the tendency to rely on readily available information when making decisions, rather than seeking out more comprehensive or accurate information. In financial decision-making, individuals may be influenced by recent market trends, news headlines, or the experiences of friends and family. Recognizing the limitations of the availability heuristic encourages individuals to conduct thorough research and analysis before making financial choices.

Overconfidence bias involves an individual's overestimation of their own abilities, leading to excessive risk-taking and a lack of consideration for potential downsides. Overconfidence can contribute to investment mistakes, financial losses, and missed opportunities. Cultivating humility and a realistic self-assessment are key to mitigating the impact of overconfidence on financial decisions.

As individuals navigate the complex landscape of financial decision-making, it's essential to recognize the interplay between emotions, cognitive biases, and rational thinking. Striking a balance between emotional awareness and logical reasoning is crucial for making sound financial choices that align with long-term goals and values.

Financial education and awareness play a pivotal role in equipping individuals with the knowledge and tools needed to navigate the emotional and cognitive aspects of money. Schools, employers, and community organizations can contribute to financial literacy initiatives that empower individuals to make informed decisions, manage emotions, and build resilient financial futures.

In addition to individual decision-making, the emotional relationship with money extends to broader economic phenomena. Market sentiment, investor behavior, and consumer confidence are influenced by collective emotions and perceptions. Economic cycles, market bubbles, and financial crises are often fueled by a combination of individual and collective emotional responses to economic events.

Understanding the emotional underpinnings of economic phenomena is essential for policymakers, central banks, and financial institutions. Monetary and fiscal policies are crafted with the goal of stabilizing economies, managing inflation, and fostering economic growth. However, the success of these policies depends, in part, on how individuals and businesses respond emotionally to economic conditions.

For example, during periods of economic uncertainty, individuals may choose to hoard cash, reduce spending, and delay major financial decisions. These collective behaviors can amplify economic downturns, contributing to a self-reinforcing cycle of reduced consumer spending and business investment. On the contrary, periods of economic optimism may lead to increased consumer spending, investment, and economic expansion

The Money Mindset Spectrum

Money mindsets and attitudes encompass a diverse spectrum of beliefs, values, and behaviors that individuals hold regarding finances. These mindsets shape the way people approach earning, spending, saving, and investing money. Understanding the various money mindsets provides insights into the factors influencing financial decisions and can be instrumental in fostering financial well-being. From scarcity mindsets to abundance mentalities, from risk-averse attitudes to entrepreneurial spirits, each money mindset reflects a unique perspective on wealth and financial success.

The scarcity mindset is characterized by a belief that resources, including money, are limited and finite. Individuals with a scarcity mindset often feel a constant sense of financial insecurity and may adopt frugal habits out of fear of running out of money. This mindset can lead to a reluctance to take risks or invest in opportunities, as individuals may prioritize hoarding resources over potential growth. Overcoming a scarcity mindset involves shifting towards an abundance mentality, recognizing opportunities for growth, and embracing a positive outlook on financial possibilities.

In contrast to the scarcity mindset, an abundance mindset is rooted in the belief that opportunities and resources are plentiful. Those with an abundance mentality view money as a flowing and renewable resource, allowing them to approach financial decisions with optimism and confidence. This mindset encourages individuals to explore investment opportunities, take calculated risks, and embrace a more expansive view of wealth. Cultivating an abundance mindset involves reframing negative thoughts about scarcity and adopting a mindset of gratitude and abundance.

A risk-averse attitude reflects a preference for safety and stability in financial decisions. Individuals with this mindset prioritize preserving capital and avoiding potential losses. While risk aversion can protect against financial setbacks, it may also limit opportunities for growth and wealth accumulation. Striking a balance between risk and reward involves understanding one's risk tolerance, diversifying investments, and making informed decisions based on a realistic assessment of potential outcomes.

On the opposite end of the spectrum is the risk-taking mentality, where individuals are more inclined to embrace uncertainty and pursue high-risk, high-reward opportunities. This mindset is often associated with entrepreneurs, investors, and individuals seeking rapid financial growth. While a risk-taking mentality can lead to significant success, it also carries the potential for substantial losses. Managing risk involves thorough research, strategic planning, and a willingness to learn from both successes and failures.

A consumerist mindset centers around the belief that happiness and fulfillment come from acquiring material possessions and indulging in lifestyle choices. Individuals with a strong consumerist mindset may prioritize spending on luxury items, experiences, and status symbols. While this mindset can provide immediate gratification, it may contribute to financial stress, debt accumulation, and a lack of long-term financial planning. Shifting towards a more intentional and value-based approach to spending involves aligning purchases with personal values and long-term goals.

The saver's mentality is characterized by a strong inclination towards saving and building financial reserves. Individuals with this mindset prioritize financial security, emergency funds, and long-term savings goals. While saving is a fundamental aspect of financial health, an extreme saver's mentality may lead to missed investment opportunities and a reluctance to enjoy the fruits of one's labor. Balancing saving with strategic spending and investing is key to achieving both short-term and long-term financial objectives.

The entrepreneurial spirit embodies a mindset that seeks opportunities for innovation, wealth creation, and financial independence. Entrepreneurs often possess a high tolerance for risk, a willingness to challenge the status quo, and a desire to build and grow businesses. This mindset goes beyond traditional employment and embraces the idea of creating value and generating income through entrepreneurial endeavors. Fostering an entrepreneurial spirit involves cultivating creativity, resilience, and a proactive approach to identifying and pursuing opportunities.

In contrast to the entrepreneurial spirit, the employee mindset reflects a preference for stable employment, job security, and a steady income. Individuals with this mindset may prioritize the benefits of traditional employment, such as a regular salary, benefits, and a structured work environment. While the employee mindset provides stability, it may limit financial independence and the potential for significant wealth accumulation. Finding a balance between stability and entrepreneurial pursuits can lead to a more holistic approach to financial success.

The generosity and philanthropy mindset center around the belief that wealth should be used to make a positive impact on others and society. Individuals with this mindset prioritize giving back, supporting charitable causes, and making a difference in the lives of others. While generosity is a noble value, it requires thoughtful planning to ensure that giving aligns with personal values and does not compromise one's financial well-being. Incorporating philanthropy into financial planning involves setting aside funds for charitable contributions and aligning giving with broader financial goals.

The FIRE mindset is characterized by a strong desire for financial independence and early retirement. Individuals embracing the FIRE movement prioritize aggressive saving, frugal living, and strategic investing to achieve financial freedom at an early age. While the FIRE mindset offers a compelling vision of early retirement, it requires disciplined financial habits and a commitment to prioritizing long-term goals over immediate gratification. Balancing the pursuit of financial independence with a fulfilling and meaningful life is essential for those following the FIRE philosophy.

A debt-averse approach reflects a strong aversion to borrowing money and accumulating debt. Individuals with this mindset prioritize living within their means, avoiding credit cards, and paying off debts as quickly as possible. While a debt-averse approach promotes financial discipline, it may also limit opportunities for leveraging credit for investments or strategic financial moves. Understanding the difference between healthy and detrimental debt and making informed borrowing decisions is crucial for achieving financial goals.

The financial resilience and adaptability mindset emphasize the ability to navigate and bounce back from financial challenges. Individuals with this mindset view setbacks as opportunities for growth, learn from failures, and adapt their financial strategies to changing circumstances. Cultivating financial resilience involves developing a proactive approach to financial planning, building emergency funds, and embracing a mindset of continuous learning and adaptation.

A family-centric attitude revolves around the belief that family and relationships take precedence over individual financial goals. Individuals with this mindset prioritize providing for their families, supporting children's education, and creating a legacy for future generations. While family-centric attitudes foster strong social bonds, it requires careful financial planning to balance individual and family goals, ensuring that both are addressed in a sustainable manner.

The minimalist mindset centers on the belief that happiness and fulfillment come from simplifying life, decluttering possessions, and prioritizing experiences over material possessions. Individuals with this mindset may intentionally limit their spending, focus on essential needs, and seek a more intentional and meaningful lifestyle. While minimalism can lead to financial freedom, it requires a conscious effort to resist societal pressures and redefine the relationship with material possessions.

The traditionalist approach reflects adherence to conventional financial norms and practices. Individuals with this mindset may follow traditional paths of education, employment, homeownership, and retirement planning. While a traditionalist approach provides a sense of stability, it may also limit exploration of alternative

Identifying your own money mindset is a crucial step toward understanding the beliefs, values, and behaviors that shape your financial decisions. Your money mindset influences how you earn, spend, save, and invest money, and recognizing it provides valuable insights into your relationship with finances. Here are key steps to help you identify and understand your money mindset:

Begin by reflecting on your upbringing and the financial attitudes and behaviors modeled by your family. Consider the messages you received about money during childhood and how they may have influenced your current mindset. Were there specific beliefs or values regarding saving, spending, or investing that were ingrained in you? Understanding your financial upbringing can uncover the roots of your money mindset.

Take a close look at your current financial habits and behaviors. How do you approach budgeting, spending, and saving? Are you a natural saver, or do you tend to spend impulsively? Do you view debt as a tool for achieving goals, or are you debt-averse? Analyzing your day-to-day financial decisions provides valuable clues about your underlying money mindset.

Assess your attitudes toward risk and uncertainty in financial matters. Are you comfortable taking risks in investments, or do you prefer safer, more conservative approaches? Understanding your risk tolerance is a key aspect of identifying your money mindset, as it influences your investment choices and overall financial strategy.

Reflect on your financial goals and priorities. What do you aspire to achieve with your money? Whether it's financial independence, homeownership, travel, or philanthropy, your goals reflect your values and aspirations. Identifying your priorities provides insights into the motivations driving your financial decisions.

Pay attention to your emotional responses when it comes to money. How do you feel about financial setbacks, windfalls, or unexpected expenses? Emotions such as fear, joy, stress, or contentment can reveal underlying attitudes and beliefs about money. Recognizing these emotional responses is essential for gaining a holistic understanding of your money mindset.

Consider your views on success and wealth. What does financial success mean to you? Is it defined by a specific income level, material possessions, or a sense of financial security? Your definition of success reflects your values and influences the financial choices you make.

Assess your relationship with debt. How do you approach borrowing money, and what purpose does debt serve in your financial strategy? Whether you see debt as a helpful tool or something to be avoided, your attitude toward borrowing provides insights into your overall money mindset.

Consider the influence of societal and cultural norms

on your money mindset. Are you influenced by external expectations, such as keeping up with a certain lifestyle or adhering to societal benchmarks? Understanding the external pressures that shape your financial attitudes helps differentiate between societal expectations and your personal values.

Engage in conversations about money with trusted friends, family, or financial advisors. Seeking feedback and different perspectives can provide valuable external insights into your money mindset. Others may offer observations or perspectives that you may not have considered, contributing to a more comprehensive understanding of your financial attitudes.

Take the time to educate yourself about money psychology, including various money mindsets and the psychological factors influencing financial decisions. Understanding the broader landscape of money attitudes can help you contextualize your own mindset and identify areas for personal growth and development.

By undertaking these steps, you can gain a clearer understanding of your money mindset and how it shapes your financial decisions. This self-awareness forms the foundation for making intentional and informed choices that align with your values, goals, and overall financial well-being. Remember that money mindsets are dynamic and can evolve over time, so regularly revisiting and reassessing your beliefs about money is a valuable practice on your financial journey.

Money Memories and Childhood

Childhood experiences play a pivotal role in shaping our money beliefs and attitudes. The formative years of our lives, during which we absorb lessons, values, and behaviors from our families and surroundings, have a lasting impact on how we view and interact with money. These early experiences contribute to the development of our money mindset, influencing our financial decisions, habits, and emotions throughout adulthood.

One of the most significant factors shaping our money beliefs is the observation of parental money behaviors. Children are keen observers, absorbing information from their parents' financial habits, attitudes toward spending, saving, and investing. If parents exhibit responsible financial behaviors, such as budgeting, saving for the future, and making informed investment decisions, children are likely to internalize these practices. Conversely, if parents display impulsive spending, financial stress, or a lack of financial planning, these behaviors may become ingrained in a child's money mindset.

The way parents communicate about money with their children also plays a crucial role. Open and transparent discussions about budgeting, saving goals, and the value of money provide children with a foundation for understanding financial principles. If parents avoid discussing money matters or communicate anxieties about financial issues, children may develop a sense of uncertainty or fear around money. Clear communication fosters financial literacy and a healthier relationship with money.

Families often have distinct financial values and priorities that influence the allocation of resources. Whether it's prioritizing education, homeownership, charitable giving, or experiences, these values shape children's perceptions of what is important in life. For example, if a family prioritizes travel and experiences, a child may grow up valuing those opportunities and may allocate resources accordingly in adulthood. Understanding the financial values instilled during childhood provides insights into personal financial priorities and decision-making.

Childhood experiences also impact attitudes toward work, success, and the connection between effort and financial reward. Children who witness hard work, resilience, and the pursuit of goals are likely to develop a strong work ethic and a belief in the correlation between effort and financial success. Conversely, if childhood experiences involve a lack of emphasis on work or achievement, individuals may struggle with motivation and goal-setting in adulthood.

Childhood experiences related to economic conditions within the family can significantly influence money beliefs. Families experiencing financial scarcity may instill a sense of frugality, resourcefulness, and the importance of saving. On the other hand, children growing up in financially abundant households may develop a more relaxed attitude toward spending and experience fewer anxieties about resource limitations. These early experiences with scarcity or abundance shape one's approach to financial decision-making later in life.

The level of financial education provided during childhood contributes to the development of money beliefs. Families that prioritize financial literacy through discussions about budgeting, investing, and the basics of personal finance empower children with the knowledge to make informed decisions. In contrast, a lack of financial education may leave individuals ill-equipped to navigate complex financial landscapes, potentially leading to challenges in adulthood.

How families handle financial challenges and crises

influences a child's perception of resilience and coping mechanisms. If parents navigate financial setbacks with resilience, adaptability, and a problem-solving mindset, children are likely to internalize these positive coping strategies. On the other hand, witnessing stress, conflict, or avoidance in the face of financial challenges may contribute to a negative emotional association with money.

The nature of gifts and rewards provided during childhood can shape attitudes toward material possessions and the value of money. Children who receive thoughtful gifts with consideration for their interests and needs may develop an appreciation for meaningful spending. On the contrary, an excessive focus on materialism or inconsistent reward systems may contribute to impulsive spending habits or a skewed perception of the relationship between effort and reward.

The level of financial stability and security within a family impacts a child's sense of safety and well-being. Children growing up in financially stable households may develop a sense of security and confidence in their financial future. In contrast, children experiencing financial instability or witnessing financial stress may internalize a sense of insecurity, leading to a more cautious and risk-averse money mindset in adulthood.

Cultural and social influences present during childhood contribute to the formation of money beliefs. Cultural norms regarding spending, saving, and investing, as well as societal expectations related to success and status, shape a child's understanding of financial behavior. For example, cultures that emphasize communal support may instill values of financial interdependence, while individualistic cultures may prioritize financial independence.

The modeling of gender roles in finances within a family can influence a child's perceptions of gender-related financial responsibilities. If traditional gender roles are reinforced, with specific expectations for how men and women handle money, these beliefs may be internalized and carried into adulthood. Challenging stereotypical gender norms can lead to more equitable and shared financial responsibilities within relationships.

Discussions or experiences related to inheritance and legacy planning can shape a child's understanding of wealth transfer and long-term financial planning. Families that openly communicate about the importance of legacy, estate planning, and wealth preservation may instill a sense of responsibility and stewardship. In contrast, a lack of communication on these topics may result in uncertainty and unpreparedness for managing inherited wealth.

Understanding how childhood experiences shape money beliefs is an essential step in developing financial self-awareness. Reflecting on these experiences allows individuals to identify both positive and negative aspects of their money mindset, enabling them to make intentional changes and cultivate a healthier relationship with money. Recognizing the influence of childhood experiences provides a foundation for breaking harmful patterns, adopting positive financial behaviors, and building a more resilient and empowered approach to personal finance.

Cognitive Biases in Financial Decision-Making

C ognitive biases play a significant role in financial decision-making, influencing how individuals process information, assess risks, and make choices related to money. These biases are systematic patterns of deviation from norm or rationality in judgment, often leading to suboptimal or irrational decisions. In the realm of personal finance, understanding cognitive biases is crucial for making informed and rational choices, managing risks, and achieving long-term financial well-being. Here, we explore several key cognitive biases that impact financial decision-making.

Loss aversion is a fundamental cognitive bias wherein individuals place more emphasis on avoiding losses than on acquiring equivalent gains. In financial decision-making, this bias can lead to risk aversion and a reluctance to make decisions that might result in losses. Investors, for example, may hold onto declining investments rather than selling at a loss due to the emotional impact of loss aversion. Overcoming this bias involves recognizing that losses are a natural part of investing and making decisions based on a rational assessment of future prospects rather than past losses.

Anchoring bias occurs when individuals rely too heavily on the first piece of information encountered (the "anchor") when making decisions. In financial contexts, individuals might anchor their judgments about the value of an asset, the price of a product, or the feasibility of an investment based on initial reference points. For instance, an investor might anchor their decision to buy a stock at a certain price, even if subsequent information suggests a different valuation.

Mitigating anchoring bias involves consciously reassessing information without being overly influenced by the initial anchor.

Confirmation bias is the tendency to interpret new evidence as confirmation of one's existing beliefs or theories while ignoring information that contradicts them. In financial decision-making, individuals may seek out information that supports their preconceived notions about investments, spending habits, or economic trends. For example, an investor with a positive outlook on a specific stock may only focus on news articles or analyses that validate their optimistic view. Overcoming confirmation bias requires actively seeking diverse perspectives, challenging assumptions, and considering information that may challenge one's existing beliefs.

Overconfidence bias involves an individual's overestimation of their own abilities, leading to excessive risk-taking and a lack of consideration for potential downsides. In financial decision-making, overconfident individuals may trade more frequently, take on too much leverage, or ignore warning signs in the market. This bias can contribute to investment mistakes, financial losses, and missed opportunities. Cultivating humility, seeking external feedback, and maintaining a realistic self-assessment are crucial for mitigating the impact of overconfidence bias.

The availability heuristic is the tendency to rely on readily available information when making decisions, rather than seeking out more comprehensive or accurate information. In the financial context, individuals may be influenced by recent market trends, news headlines, or the experiences of friends and family. For example, an investor might be swayed by a recent successful investment story without considering the broader market conditions. Overcoming the availability heuristic involves actively seeking diverse sources of information, conducting thorough research, and avoiding decisions based solely on easily accessible data.

Herd mentality, or herd behavior, refers to the tendency of individuals to follow the actions and decisions of a larger group. In financial markets, this bias can lead to asset bubbles, market panics, and excessive volatility. Investors may buy or sell assets based on the actions of others rather than conducting independent analysis. Recognizing and resisting herd mentality involves maintaining independent thinking, conducting thorough research, and making decisions based on one's own analysis rather than following the crowd.

The sunk cost fallacy is the inclination to continue investing in a project or decision based on the cumulative investment made, even when it is clear that the future costs outweigh the benefits. In financial decision-making, individuals may hold onto losing investments or continue to allocate resources to a failing project simply because they have already invested significant time or money. Overcoming the sunk cost fallacy requires a rational assessment of future prospects, focusing on future costs and benefits rather than past investments.

The framing effect occurs when the way information is presented (or "framed") influences decision-making. For instance, individuals may react differently to the same information presented in a positive frame (e.g., "90% fat-free") versus a negative frame (e.g., "10% fat"). In financial contexts, framing can impact investment decisions, with individuals responding differently to information presented positively or negatively. Being aware of framing effects and considering information from multiple perspectives can help individuals make more objective financial decisions.

The endowment effect is the tendency for individuals to assign a higher value to items they own simply because they own them. In financial decision-making, this bias can lead to reluctance in selling assets at market prices, as individuals may overvalue what they possess. Investors, for example, may hold onto underperforming stocks due to the emotional attachment associated with ownership. Overcoming the endowment effect involves recognizing the intrinsic value of assets and making decisions based on current market conditions.

Recency bias is the tendency to give more weight to recent events or information when making decisions. In financial markets, individuals influenced by recency bias may extrapolate recent trends into the future, leading to buying or selling decisions based on short-term movements. For instance, after a period of market volatility, investors may become overly pessimistic about future returns. Mitigating recency bias involves considering historical data, long-term trends, and avoiding knee-jerk reactions based on recent events.

The Dunning-Kruger effect refers to the cognitive bias where individuals with low ability at a task overestimate their ability. In financial decision-making, this bias can manifest when individuals with limited financial knowledge believe they have a deep understanding of complex financial concepts. Recognizing the limits of one's knowledge, seeking education, and consulting with financial professionals can help mitigate the impact of the Dunning-Kruger effect.

Optimism bias involves individuals consistently overestimating the likelihood of positive events and underestimating the likelihood of negative events. In finance, individuals may be overly optimistic about the potential returns of an investment or underestimate the risks involved. Managing optimism bias requires a realistic assessment of potential outcomes, consideration of downside risks, and a balanced approach to decision-making.

Regret aversion is the fear of making decisions that may lead to subsequent regret. In financial decision-making, individuals may avoid taking necessary risks or making investment decisions due to the fear of regretting a wrong choice. This bias can result in missed opportunities and suboptimal financial outcomes. Overcoming regret aversion involves recognizing that not all decisions will be perfect and making choices based on informed analysis rather than a fear of potential regret.

Behavioral finance encompasses various biases that influence financial decision-making. These include the disposition effect (tendency to sell winning investments and hold onto losing ones), the house money effect (willingness to take greater risks after a recent gain), and the mental accounting bias (segmenting money into different categories with varying risk tolerances). Understanding these behavioral finance biases is crucial for making decisions

Financial Goals and Motivation

Financial goals and motivation are integral components of personal finance, shaping the way individuals plan, manage, and achieve their financial aspirations. Whether aiming for short-term objectives like paying off debt or pursuing long-term goals such as retirement planning, understanding the dynamics of financial goals and motivation is essential for building a solid foundation for financial well-being. In this exploration, we delve into the significance of financial goals, the factors that influence motivation, and effective strategies for aligning aspirations with actions.

Financial goals serve as compass points, providing direction and purpose to individual financial decisions. Whether it's budgeting, saving, or investing, having clear goals helps individuals prioritize and allocate resources effectively. Without defined goals, financial decisions may lack a strategic framework, leading to scattered efforts and suboptimal outcomes.

Financial goals act as a roadmap, outlining the journey from the current financial state to the desired future. A well-defined roadmap helps individuals set milestones, track progress, and make necessary adjustments along the way. This structured approach enhances the likelihood of success by breaking down large objectives into manageable steps.

Financial goals serve as powerful motivators, providing individuals with a compelling reason to take action and exercise financial discipline. The prospect of achieving a goal, whether it's buying a home, starting a business, or funding education, fuels the motivation needed to make consistent, positive financial choices.

Well-crafted financial goals contribute to building financial resilience. By setting aside funds for emergencies, establishing an emergency fund, and planning for unexpected expenses, individuals create a financial safety net. This resilience helps weather economic uncertainties and unexpected challenges, fostering a sense of financial security.

Setting and pursuing financial goals require a deep understanding of one's financial situation. This heightened financial awareness empowers individuals to make informed decisions, understand the implications of financial choices, and cultivate a proactive approach to money management.

Financial goals enable individuals to align their spending habits with their values and priorities. By identifying and prioritizing what matters most, individuals can allocate resources to areas that bring true fulfillment and satisfaction. This alignment contributes to a sense of purpose in financial decision-making.

Long-term wealth accumulation is often a fundamental financial goal, whether for retirement, legacy planning, or achieving financial freedom. Setting and working toward these goals involve strategic investment, savings, and wealth-building strategies that contribute to sustained financial success over time.

Intrinsic motivation stems from internal desires, personal values, and a sense of accomplishment. Individuals driven by intrinsic motivation find fulfillment in achieving goals for the sake of personal growth and satisfaction. Financial goals aligned with personal values often tap into intrinsic motivation, fostering a lasting commitment to the pursuit of those objectives.

Extrinsic motivation is derived from external factors such as rewards, recognition, or social approval. External motivators, like earning a bonus, receiving accolades for financial achievements, or gaining recognition from peers, can drive individuals to pursue financial goals. However, relying solely on extrinsic motivation may lead to a lack of sustained commitment if external rewards diminish.

Fear can be a powerful motivator in financial decision-making. The fear of financial instability, debt, or not achieving essential goals may drive individuals to take proactive steps toward financial security. While fear can be a potent initial motivator, a balanced approach involves channeling these emotions into positive actions and long-term planning.

The desire for financial independence often serves as a compelling motivator. Achieving a level of financial autonomy allows individuals to make choices based on personal fulfillment rather than financial necessity. This motivation extends beyond immediate needs and contributes to long-term financial planning and wealth-building.

Social comparisons and peer influence play a role in motivating financial decisions. Observing the financial successes of peers or desiring a certain lifestyle based on societal expectations can drive individuals to set and pursue specific financial goals. While external comparisons can be motivating, it's essential to ensure that goals align with individual values and aspirations.

Recognizing the future benefits of achieving financial goals can be a strong motivator. Whether it's envisioning a comfortable retirement, a debt-free life, or the ability to pursue passions without financial constraints, a clear vision of the positive outcomes motivates individuals to make disciplined financial choices in the present.

Financial goals often involve personal growth and development. Individuals motivated by the prospect of self-improvement, acquiring new skills, or realizing their full potential may find that financial goals serve as catalysts for continuous learning and development.

Financial goals that align with one's life values and overarching life purpose are more likely to elicit sustained motivation. Whether prioritizing family, education, philanthropy, or other values, aligning financial goals with these core principles enhances the sense of purpose and commitment to the journey.

Financial education and awareness contribute to motivation by providing individuals with the knowledge and tools needed to make informed decisions. Understanding the impact of financial choices, investment strategies, and the long-term consequences of financial decisions enhances motivation. Financial literacy empowers individuals to navigate complex financial landscapes, make sound choices, and stay motivated on the path toward achieving their goals.

Clarity is key to maintaining motivation. Clearly define your financial goals, making them specific, measurable, achievable, relevant, and time-bound (SMART). For example, instead of a vague goal like "save money," set a specific goal like "save $5,000 for an emergency fund by the end of the year." Clear objectives provide a roadmap and milestones for tracking progress.

Prioritizing financial goals helps manage focus and resources effectively. Identify the most critical goals that align with your values and have a significant impact on your financial well-being. By prioritizing, you can allocate resources efficiently and avoid spreading efforts too thin.

Large, intimidating goals can be overwhelming. Break them down into smaller, actionable steps. Create a step-by-step plan with achievable tasks. Celebrate each small victory along the way, reinforcing the sense of progress and motivation.

Visualization is a powerful tool for maintaining motivation. Envision the positive outcomes of achieving your financial goals. Whether it's picturing debt-free living, a comfortable retirement, or pursuing a passion without financial constraints, visualizing success can reinforce motivation and provide a clear vision of the benefits.

A financial vision board is a visual representation of your financial goals and aspirations. Use images, quotes, and symbols to represent the lifestyle, achievements, and financial milestones you aim to reach. Placing the vision board in a visible location serves as a daily reminder and motivates you to stay committed to your financial journey.

Financial goals are not static; they may need adjustment based on changing circumstances, priorities, or external factors. Regularly review your goals, assess progress, and make adjustments as needed. Flexibility ensures that your goals remain relevant and achievable, sustaining motivation over the long term.

Celebrate your financial achievements, regardless of size. Acknowledging and rewarding progress reinforces positive behavior. Whether it's paying off a credit card, reaching a savings milestone, or making successful investments, celebrate these victories to maintain motivation and build momentum.

Sharing your financial goals with a trusted friend, family member, or financial advisor can provide accountability and support. An accountability partner can offer encouragement, share insights, and help you stay on track during challenging times. Jointly pursuing financial goals can enhance motivation through mutual support.

Financial education is an ongoing process. Stay informed about personal finance, investment strategies, and economic trends. Continuous learning not only enhances your financial knowledge but also boosts confidence, empowering you to make informed decisions and stay motivated.

Embrace a growth mindset that views challenges as opportunities for learning and growth. Understand that setbacks are part of the financial journey and use them as learning experiences. A growth mindset fosters resilience, adaptability, and a positive outlook, contributing to sustained financial motivation.

Financial journeys can be filled with ups and downs. Practice self-compassion and avoid self-criticism in moments of financial challenges. Treat yourself with kindness, recognize that everyone faces setbacks, and focus on learning and improving rather than dwelling on mistakes.

Regularly revisit your core values and ensure that your financial goals align with them. When goals are connected to your values, they become more meaningful and motivating. Consider how achieving your financial aspirations contributes to a life that reflects your deepest values and priorities.

Engage with communities or groups that share similar financial goals. Whether online or offline, being part of a supportive community provides encouragement, shared experiences, and insights. Knowing that others are facing similar challenges and celebrating similar successes can enhance your motivation.

If navigating complex financial decisions becomes overwhelming, consider seeking professional guidance. Financial advisors can provide expertise, personalized strategies, and tailored advice. Their support can instill confidence, address uncertainties, and help you stay motivated on your financial path.

Financial goals and motivation form the cornerstone of a sound financial plan, guiding individuals toward a future of financial well-being and security. The interplay between setting clear goals and staying motivated involves understanding personal values, leveraging intrinsic and extrinsic motivators, and adopting effective strategies for goal attainment. By aligning financial aspirations with intentional actions, individuals can cultivate a mindset of continuous improvement, resilience, and long-term success in their financial endeavors.

Regular reflection, adjustment, and a commitment to lifelong learning contribute to a dynamic and sustainable approach to achieving financial goals. Ultimately, the journey towards financial success is a personal and transformative experience that goes beyond the mere accumulation of wealth—it is about creating a life that reflects one's values, passions, and aspirations.

Spending and Saving Habits

Spending and saving habits play a pivotal role in shaping an individual's financial well-being. The way individuals allocate their money—whether through spending on necessities, discretionary purchases, or saving for the future —has a profound impact on their financial health, goals, and overall quality of life. In this exploration, we delve into the dynamics of spending and saving habits, examining the factors that influence these behaviors, the consequences they entail, and strategies for fostering healthy financial practices.

Spending habits are shaped by a myriad of factors, including:

Income Levels: The amount of income an individual earns significantly influences spending habits. Higher income levels may afford more discretionary spending, while lower income levels may necessitate more strategic budgeting.

Lifestyle Choices: Personal preferences, lifestyle choices, and values play a crucial role in spending habits. Individuals may allocate funds differently based on priorities such as travel, entertainment, health, or experiences.

Cultural Influences: Cultural norms, societal expectations, and regional influences contribute to spending behaviors. Different cultures may emphasize specific spending priorities, impacting individuals' choices regarding housing, transportation, and leisure.

Peer Pressure and Social Comparisons: The desire to fit in or keep up with peers can influence spending decisions. Social comparisons and the pressure to conform to certain standards may drive individuals to spend on status symbols or lifestyle choices.

Psychological Factors: Emotional and psychological factors, such as stress, boredom, or the need for instant gratification, can lead to impulsive spending. Understanding and managing these psychological triggers is crucial for fostering healthy spending habits.

Advertising and Marketing: The constant exposure to advertising and marketing messages can shape consumer preferences and influence spending habits. Effective marketing campaigns may create perceived needs, leading to increased spending on specific products or services.

Spending habits can be categorized into various types, reflecting different approaches to money management:

Impulse Spending: This involves making unplanned purchases on a whim, often driven by emotions or external influences. Impulse spending can lead to financial strain and undermine long-term financial goals.

Frugal Spending: Frugal spending involves a conscious effort to prioritize needs over wants, seeking value for money, and minimizing unnecessary expenses. Frugal individuals focus on mindful consumption and avoiding unnecessary debt.

Conspicuous Consumption: This spending habit centers on displaying wealth and social status through visible, often extravagant, purchases. Individuals engaging in conspicuous consumption may prioritize the appearance of affluence over long-term financial security.

Budget-Conscious Spending: Individuals with budget-conscious spending habits carefully plan and allocate funds based on a predefined budget. This approach promotes financial discipline and ensures that spending aligns with financial goals.

Experiential Spending: Some individuals prioritize spending on experiences rather than material possessions. Experiential spending focuses on creating memories and enjoying life rather than accumulating tangible assets.

Routine Spending: Routine spending involves regular, recurring expenses for necessities such as housing, utilities, groceries, and transportation. While essential, managing routine spending effectively is crucial for financial stability.

Unhealthy spending habits can have far-reaching consequences, impacting various aspects of an individual's financial and personal life:

Accumulation of Debt: Excessive and impulsive spending often leads to the accumulation of debt, whether through credit cards, personal loans, or other forms of borrowing. High-interest debt can become a significant financial burden.

Financial Stress: Uncontrolled spending can result in financial stress, as individuals struggle to meet their financial obligations, leading to anxiety, sleep disturbances, and overall reduced well-being.

Impaired Savings: Insufficient focus on saving can hinder progress toward financial goals such as homeownership, education, or retirement. Inadequate savings can leave individuals vulnerable to unexpected expenses or economic downturns.

Limited Investment Opportunities: Consistently high spending with minimal savings may limit opportunities for investments that could contribute to long-term wealth accumulation. Investments play a crucial role in building financial security over time.

Strained Relationships: Financial disagreements are a common source of tension in relationships. Divergent spending habits and financial priorities can strain personal relationships, leading to conflict and dissatisfaction.

Reduced Future Opportunities: Unhealthy spending habits may limit opportunities for personal and professional growth. Lack of financial resources can hinder educational pursuits, career advancements, or entrepreneurial ventures.

Saving habits are influenced by a range of factors, and individuals' attitudes toward saving are shaped by a combination of personal, societal, and economic influences:

Financial Literacy: Individuals with a higher level of financial literacy tend to have better saving habits. Understanding the importance of saving, investment opportunities, and the power of compounding motivates individuals to prioritize saving.

Income Stability: The stability of income impacts an individual's ability to save consistently. Those with irregular or unpredictable income may find it challenging to establish a steady savings routine.

Future Goals and Aspirations: Saving habits are closely tied to future goals and aspirations. Whether saving for a home, education, travel, or retirement, having clear goals provides motivation and purpose for saving.

Emergency Preparedness: The awareness of the importance of an emergency fund influences saving habits. Individuals who prioritize building a financial safety net are more likely to adopt consistent saving practices.

Cultural and Family Influences: Cultural norms and family traditions regarding saving contribute to individual saving habits. Upbringing and familial attitudes toward money often shape an individual's approach to saving.

Economic Conditions: Economic conditions, such as inflation rates and interest rates, can impact saving habits. Low-interest environments may discourage traditional savings, while economic uncertainties may encourage a focus on building financial reserves.

Saving habits encompass various approaches to setting aside money for future needs:

Regular Savings: Regular savings involve setting aside a fixed amount of money at regular intervals, such as monthly or bi-weekly. This disciplined approach promotes consistency in building financial reserves.

Automated Savings: Automated savings involve setting up automatic transfers from a checking account to a savings account. This hands-off approach ensures that a portion of income is saved without the need for manual intervention.

Goal-Specific Savings: Individuals may adopt goal-specific savings habits, allocating funds toward particular objectives such as a down payment for a home, education expenses, or a dream vacation. This approach provides focus and motivation.

Emergency Fund Saving: Establishing an emergency fund is a specific saving habit aimed at creating a financial buffer for unexpected expenses or income disruptions. Emergency fund savings contribute to financial resilience.

Retirement Savings: Saving for retirement is a long-term saving habit that involves systematically contributing to retirement accounts such as 401(k)s, IRAs, or pension plans. Consistent retirement savings are essential for financial security in later years.

Investment Savings: Beyond traditional savings, individuals may adopt a habit of investing to grow their wealth. Investment savings involve allocating funds to diverse investment vehicles with the goal of generating returns over time.

Cultivating healthy saving habits yields a multitude of benefits that contribute to an individual's financial well-being and overall financial success:

Financial Security: Healthy saving habits provide a financial safety net, offering protection against unexpected expenses, emergencies, or income disruptions. This sense of financial security contributes to peace of mind and reduces stress.

Goal Achievement: Saving habits aligned with specific goals facilitate the achievement of those objectives. Whether saving for a home, education, travel, or retirement, consistent saving brings individuals closer to realizing their aspirations.

Emergency Preparedness: Establishing and maintaining an emergency fund through saving habits ensures preparedness for unforeseen financial challenges. An emergency fund provides a cushion to cover unexpected expenses without resorting to debt.

Opportunity for Investments: Saving regularly creates opportunities for investments, allowing individuals to grow their wealth over time. Investments offer the potential for higher returns than traditional savings accounts, contributing to long-term financial goals.

Debt Avoidance or Reduction: Healthy saving habits can serve as a preventive measure against accumulating debt. Having savings allows individuals to cover expenses without resorting to borrowing, reducing reliance on credit cards or loans.

Financial Independence: Consistent saving habits contribute to financial independence, allowing individuals to make choices based on personal preferences rather than financial necessity. This independence enhances overall well-being and quality of life.

Retirement Readiness: Regular contributions to retirement savings accounts ensure readiness for retirement. Healthy saving habits in this regard provide financial security during post-employment years, allowing individuals to enjoy a comfortable retirement lifestyle.

Stress Reduction: Financial stress is often alleviated through disciplined saving habits. Knowing that there are financial reserves for emergencies and future goals reduces anxiety and fosters a positive relationship with money.

Flexibility and Adaptability: Saving habits instill financial flexibility, enabling individuals to adapt to changing circumstances or seize unexpected opportunities. Having savings provides a financial buffer for adapting to life transitions or pursuing new endeavors.

Establishing a budget is a fundamental step in cultivating healthy spending and saving habits. A budget outlines income, expenses, and savings goals, providing a clear roadmap for financial decision-making. Regularly review and adjust the budget based on changing circumstances.

Differentiating between needs and wants is crucial for mindful spending. Prioritize essential needs such as housing, utilities, and groceries, and allocate discretionary funds intentionally. Understanding the difference helps control impulsive spending.

Define clear, realistic, and specific financial goals. Whether short-term or long-term, having well-defined objectives provides motivation for saving and guides spending decisions. Break down larger goals into manageable steps for continuous progress.

Automate savings by setting up automatic transfers to a savings account. Automation ensures consistency and eliminates the need for manual intervention. It's an effective way to make saving a routine part of financial management.

Prioritize building an emergency fund to cover unforeseen expenses. Aim for three to six months' worth of living expenses in an easily accessible account. An emergency fund serves as a financial cushion and reduces the reliance on credit during unexpected situations.

Cultivate the habit of delayed gratification by resisting impulsive purchases. Take time to consider the necessity of a purchase, especially for non-essential items. Delaying gratification allows for thoughtful decision-making and reduces unnecessary spending.

Periodically assess spending and saving habits to ensure alignment with financial goals. Identify areas for improvement, celebrate successes, and make adjustments based on changing priorities or circumstances.

Consider consulting with a financial advisor to receive personalized guidance. Financial professionals can provide insights, recommend strategies, and assist in creating a tailored plan for achieving specific financial goals.

Enhance financial literacy through education and awareness. Stay informed about personal finance concepts, investment options, and economic trends. Continuous learning empowers individuals to make informed decisions and adapt to evolving financial landscapes.

Negotiate prices when possible and practice comparison shopping before making significant purchases. Being proactive in seeking the best deals helps stretch the budget and ensures value for money.

If applicable, involve family members in financial discussions and goal-setting. Collaborative financial planning promotes shared responsibility and ensures that everyone is aligned with the family's financial priorities.

Cultivate mindfulness in financial habits by staying present and aware of spending choices. Mindful spending involves being conscious of the impact of financial decisions on long-term goals and overall well-being.

Keep track of credit reports and scores regularly. Monitoring credit helps identify any discrepancies or issues that may impact financial stability. A good credit history is crucial for accessing favorable financial opportunities.

Join communities or groups that share similar financial goals and values. Engaging with like-minded individuals provides support, encouragement, and shared experiences, fostering a positive environment for financial growth.

Spending and saving habits are integral components of personal finance that significantly influence an individual's financial health and future prospects. Cultivating healthy habits involves a balance between mindful spending, intentional saving, and a continuous commitment to financial well-being. By understanding the factors that influence spending and saving decisions, individuals can make informed choices that align with their values and goals. Implementing effective strategies, such as budgeting, goal-setting, and automation, contributes to the development of sustainable financial practices. Ultimately, the cultivation of healthy spending and saving habits.

Mindful Spending and Conscious Consumption

Mindful spending and conscious consumption represent a paradigm shift in the way individuals approach their financial decisions and consumer behaviors. These concepts advocate for a heightened awareness of the impact of spending choices on personal well-being, the environment, and society at large. In this exploration, we delve into the principles of mindful spending and conscious consumption, examining their psychological underpinnings, the environmental and social implications, and practical strategies for incorporating mindfulness into financial habits.

Mindfulness, rooted in ancient contemplative practices, involves cultivating a heightened awareness of the present moment without judgment. Applied to spending, mindfulness encourages individuals to bring conscious attention to their financial choices, fostering a deeper understanding of needs, desires, and the motivations behind purchasing decisions.

At its core, mindful spending is about making intentional and value-driven choices. It requires individuals to pause, reflect, and assess whether a purchase aligns with their core values and contributes to their overall well-being. Mindful spending acknowledges the emotional and psychological aspects of consumer behavior, emphasizing a more deliberate and considered approach to financial decisions.

Mindful spending challenges automatic and impulsive spending habits. In a world dominated by fast-paced consumerism, individuals often make purchases without conscious thought. Mindfulness interrupts these automatic patterns, providing an opportunity for individuals to question the necessity and true value of their spending choices.

Practicing mindful spending is closely linked to cultivating gratitude and contentment. By appreciating what one already possesses and acknowledging moments of fulfillment that extend beyond material possessions, individuals can reduce the desire for excessive consumption and find satisfaction in simpler, non-material aspects of life.

Conscious consumption goes beyond individual spending habits; it encompasses a broader perspective that considers the ethical, environmental, and social implications of consumer choices. It involves making informed decisions that prioritize sustainability, ethical production practices, and the well-being of communities affected by the supply chain.

Conscious consumption emphasizes the importance of ethical and sustainable choices. This involves opting for products and services that align with environmental stewardship, fair labor practices, and social responsibility. From eco-friendly products to fair-trade goods, conscious consumers actively seek options that minimize negative impacts on the planet and society.

Conscious consumers choose to support brands and businesses committed to responsible practices. This includes transparency in sourcing, fair wages, and corporate social responsibility. By aligning their spending with ethical companies, individuals contribute to a market demand for sustainability and ethical business conduct.

Mindful spending, within the context of conscious consumption, contributes to reducing the environmental footprint. Choosing products with minimal packaging, supporting local and sustainable agriculture, and opting for durable goods that minimize waste are ways in which individuals can make eco-conscious choices through their spending habits.

Mindful spending requires emotional intelligence—the ability to recognize and understand one's emotions and their impact on decision-making. By developing emotional intelligence, individuals can make financial choices that align with their values rather than succumbing to impulsive or emotionally driven spending.

Both mindful spending and conscious consumption involve the practice of delayed gratification. Individuals consciously choose to delay immediate desires for the sake of long-term goals, whether personal, environmental, or societal. This mindset requires discipline and a shift away from instant gratification culture.

Mindful spending confronts cognitive dissonance— the discomfort arising from conflicting beliefs and actions. Individuals may experience cognitive dissonance when their spending choices conflict with their stated values. Mindfulness prompts individuals to address this discomfort, leading to more aligned and consistent financial behaviors.

Consumer identity, or the association of one's self-worth with material possessions, is a psychological aspect that mindful spending challenges. By encouraging individuals to detach their sense of identity from consumerism, mindful spending promotes a healthier and more balanced view of self-worth beyond material accumulation.

Mindful spending begins with intentional budgeting. Individuals can allocate funds based on their values and priorities, ensuring that each spending category reflects their goals and aspirations. Regularly revisiting and adjusting the budget reinforces mindful financial habits.

Before making purchases, creating a shopping list mindfully is a practical strategy. This involves thoughtfully considering needs versus wants, prioritizing essential items, and eliminating impulse purchases. A well-thought-out list guides individuals in making conscious and intentional choices.

The 24-hour rule is a mindfulness technique that involves delaying non-essential purchases for a day. This time allows individuals to reflect on the necessity and significance of the purchase. If, after 24 hours, the desire remains, the individual can make a more informed and intentional decision.

Technology plays a significant role in modern consumerism, and individuals can leverage it mindfully. Using shopping apps that provide information on product origins, ethical practices, and consumer reviews empowers individuals to make more informed and conscious choices.

Conscious consumption addresses the environmental and social impact of fast fashion. Choosing quality over quantity, supporting sustainable and ethical fashion brands, and embracing a minimalist approach contribute to a reduction in the negative consequences associated with the fast fashion industry.

Conscious consumption extends to food choices, with an emphasis on supporting local and sustainable agriculture. Individuals can choose locally sourced, organic, and ethically produced food items, reducing the environmental impact of large-scale industrial agriculture.

The conscious consumption of technology involves considering the environmental and social implications of electronic devices. Choosing products with minimal environmental impact, supporting companies committed to responsible e-waste management, and extending the lifespan of electronic devices through proper maintenance align with the principles of conscious consumption.

Conscious consumers play a pivotal role in advocating for fair labor practices. Supporting companies that prioritize fair wages, safe working conditions, and ethical labor practices encourages a shift toward more socially responsible business models.

One challenge of conscious consumption is the accessibility and affordability of ethically produced and sustainable products. Critics argue that such choices may be limited and cost-prohibitive, making it challenging for individuals with lower incomes to participate in conscious consumption fully.

Greenwashing, or the deceptive marketing of products as environmentally friendly when they are not, poses a challenge to conscious consumption. Critics argue that some companies may engage in greenwashing, creating an illusion of ethical and sustainable practices to attract conscious consumers. This highlights the importance of transparency and thorough research when making purchasing decisions to ensure that products align with the values and principles of conscious consumption.

The complexity of global supply chains presents a challenge for consumers seeking to make conscious choices. Understanding the intricate web of production, sourcing, and distribution can be overwhelming. Critics argue that achieving complete transparency in supply chains is a significant hurdle in the pursuit of truly conscious consumption.

Individuals may face challenges in balancing personal values with societal pressures. The desire to conform to societal norms, trends, or peer expectations may create tension with the principles of mindful spending and conscious consumption. Striking a balance between individual values and external influences requires self-awareness and resilience.

Cultivating mindful spending habits involves a commitment to lifelong learning and adaptation. Staying informed about evolving ethical and sustainable practices, as well as regularly reassessing personal values and financial priorities, ensures that mindful spending remains an ongoing and dynamic practice.

Instilling mindful spending habits in future generations

is a powerful way to create a lasting impact. Education systems, families, and communities can play a role in teaching the principles of mindfulness, conscious consumption, and financial literacy to ensure that these values are passed down through generations.

Mindful spending extends beyond individual habits; it involves advocating for broader systemic change. Conscious consumers can actively support and amplify initiatives that promote ethical business practices, sustainability, and corporate responsibility. Engaging in advocacy efforts contributes to a collective push for positive change.

Building a community of conscious consumers fosters collaboration and shared values. Individuals can connect with like-minded communities, participate in discussions, and collectively influence businesses and industries. Creating a network of conscious consumers amplifies the impact of mindful spending on a larger scale.

Mindful spending should be approached with sensitivity to economic realities. Individuals facing financial constraints may find it challenging to prioritize conscious consumption due to limited resources. Navigating economic constraints involves finding a balance between mindful choices and practical considerations.

Conscious consumers can advocate for and support initiatives that make ethical and sustainable options more accessible and affordable. Encouraging businesses to adopt responsible practices and offering support to initiatives that bridge the gap between affordability and ethical consumption contributes to a more inclusive conscious consumption movement.

Beyond purchasing decisions, sustainable living practices complement mindful spending. This includes reducing waste, conserving resources, and adopting eco-friendly habits. Sustainable living aligns with the principles of conscious consumption and extends the impact of mindful choices to various aspects of daily life.

Advocating for government policies that incentivize and support ethical business practices is crucial. Conscious consumers can engage in advocacy efforts to influence policy changes that promote sustainability, fair labor practices, and corporate responsibility. Collaborative efforts between consumers, businesses, and policymakers can drive systemic change.

The future of mindful spending and conscious consumption is intertwined with technological innovations that enhance transparency in supply chains. Blockchain technology, for example, has the potential to provide verifiable and transparent information about the journey of products from production to consumption, empowering consumers to make informed choices.

Increasing corporate accountability and reporting practices will likely shape the future of conscious consumption. As consumers demand transparency, businesses may be compelled to adopt more responsible practices and provide detailed information about their environmental and social impact. Reporting standards and certifications can further support these efforts.

Consumer activism and participation in social movements will continue to play a pivotal role in shaping the future of conscious consumption. Movements advocating for environmental sustainability, fair labor practices, and ethical business conduct will influence both consumer preferences and corporate behavior.

The integration of mindfulness into education can contribute to a future where conscious consumption is ingrained in societal values. Teaching mindfulness, financial literacy, and ethical decision-making in educational curricula empowers future generations to approach consumer choices with a heightened awareness of their impact.

Mindful spending and conscious consumption represent transformative approaches to financial decisions and consumer behaviors. By incorporating mindfulness into spending habits and considering the broader environmental and social implications of consumption, individuals can align their choices with personal values and contribute to positive societal change.

While challenges such as affordability, greenwashing, and complex supply chains exist, ongoing efforts in education, advocacy, and technological innovation are paving the way for a future where conscious consumption is more accessible and widespread. The commitment to lifelong learning, adaptation, and a collective shift toward ethical and sustainable practices will shape a future where mindful spending becomes an integral part of a conscious and responsible global society.

Debt and Money Stress

The psychology of debt is a complex interplay of emotions, behaviors, and cognitive processes that individuals experience when managing and dealing with financial indebtedness. Debt, whether in the form of credit cards, loans, or mortgages, goes beyond the tangible financial burden; it has profound psychological implications that can impact mental well-being, decision-making, and overall quality of life. In this exploration, we delve into the intricate aspects of the psychology of debt, examining the emotions associated with indebtedness, the cognitive processes involved, and the far-reaching impact on individuals' lives.

One of the most prevalent emotions associated with debt is stress. The burden of owing money can lead to heightened stress levels and anxiety. Individuals may constantly worry about meeting payment deadlines, managing interest rates, and avoiding financial repercussions. The fear of falling behind on payments or accumulating more debt can create a persistent state of anxiety.

Individuals in debt often experience feelings of guilt and shame. The societal stigma surrounding indebtedness can contribute to a sense of personal failure or inadequacy. The emotional weight of not meeting societal expectations or comparing oneself negatively to others who appear financially stable can exacerbate these feelings.

Chronic debt can lead to depression and feelings of despair. The persistent pressure of financial obligations, coupled with the perceived inability to break free from debt, can take a toll on mental health. Individuals may feel trapped in a cycle of despair, struggling to see a way out of their financial predicament.

Debt can evoke a sense of loss of control over one's financial situation. The inability to manage and control debt may lead to a feeling of powerlessness, contributing to stress and anxiety. Individuals may grapple with the sense that their financial destiny is dictated by external factors beyond their control.

Financial stress stemming from debt can strain relationships. Open communication about financial matters is crucial, but the emotional weight of debt may lead to avoidance or conflict. Couples may experience tension, arguments, or a breakdown in trust due to the challenges associated with indebtedness.

The shame and stigma surrounding debt may lead individuals to withdraw socially. The fear of judgment or the perception of being a financial burden on others can result in social isolation. Individuals may avoid social activities, gatherings, or discussions that involve financial aspects.

Debt can influence individuals' impulse control and decision-making. The stress and emotional toll may lead to impulsive behaviors, such as excessive spending or seeking short-term relief through more borrowing. Behavioral changes may manifest as a coping mechanism to alleviate emotional distress.

Cognitive dissonance occurs when individuals experience psychological discomfort due to conflicting beliefs or attitudes. In the context of debt, individuals may rationalize or justify their financial decisions to reduce the discomfort associated with owing money. This cognitive process can impact financial decision-making and delay efforts to address debt.

Optimism bias involves individuals underestimating the likelihood of negative events happening to them. In the context of debt, individuals may hold an optimistic belief that their financial situation will improve, leading to delayed action or avoidance of necessary steps to address indebtedness.

Time discounting refers to the tendency to place more value on immediate rewards than future benefits. In the context of debt, individuals may prioritize immediate gratification over long-term financial well-being, contributing to a cycle of short-term borrowing and delayed repayment.

Managing debt requires numerous decisions, and decision fatigue can set in when individuals face a constant barrage of financial choices. This cognitive exhaustion can lead to poor decision-making, avoidance of financial tasks, or relying on default choices that may not be in the individual's best interest.

Mental accounting involves segregating money into different mental categories based on its source or purpose. In the context of debt, individuals may engage in mental accounting by viewing different debts separately, potentially overlooking the overall financial impact. This cognitive bias can influence how individuals prioritize and address various debts.

Debt can impact career choices and professional growth. Individuals burdened by significant debt may feel constrained in pursuing career changes, entrepreneurial ventures, or further education. The financial constraints imposed by debt can limit opportunities for professional advancement.

The stress associated with debt has tangible effects on physical health. Chronic stress can contribute to conditions such as insomnia, high blood pressure, and other stress-related illnesses. The toll on physical health further exacerbates the overall impact of debt on an individual's well-being.

Debt can strain family relationships, leading to conflicts and tension. Disagreements over financial priorities, differences in spending habits, and the emotional toll of debt can contribute to marital strife and family discord. The impact is not only financial but extends to the emotional fabric of familial bonds.

Individuals in debt may face challenges in pursuing further education or personal development. The financial burden of debt can limit resources available for educational pursuits or investing in activities that contribute to personal growth.

Debt can impact the ability to achieve homeownership and housing stability. High levels of debt may hinder the ability to save for a down payment or qualify for a mortgage. Renters burdened by debt may face challenges in maintaining housing stability.

Enhancing financial literacy is a crucial step in mitigating the impact of debt. Understanding financial concepts, budgeting, and developing money management skills empower individuals to make informed decisions and take control of their financial situation.

Open communication about financial matters is essential, particularly in relationships. Couples should engage in transparent discussions about their financial situation, set joint goals, and work collaboratively to address and manage debt.

Seeking professional counseling, such as financial therapy or counseling services, can provide individuals with tools to cope with the emotional impact of debt. Mental health professionals can offer guidance on managing stress, anxiety, and emotional challenges related to financial difficulties.

Developing a strategic plan for debt repayment is crucial. Prioritize debts based on interest rates or balances and explore debt consolidation options if feasible. A structured repayment plan can provide a sense of control and progress.

Implementing a comprehensive budget and financial plan helps individuals allocate resources effectively, prioritize spending, and set aside funds for debt repayment and savings. Regularly reviewing and adjusting the budget ensures ongoing financial stability.

Building and maintaining an emergency fund is a preventive measure against unexpected expenses. An emergency fund provides a financial cushion, reducing the stress associated with unforeseen challenges.

In cases of financial hardship, negotiating with creditors can be a viable option. Exploring debt settlement, renegotiating interest rates, or arranging more favorable repayment terms may alleviate the immediate financial strain.

Mindfulness practices, such as meditation and stress-reduction techniques, can be effective in managing the emotional toll of debt. These practices promote awareness, resilience, and the ability to navigate challenges with a calm and focused mindset.

Setting realistic and achievable financial goals is essential for maintaining motivation and a sense of accomplishment. Break down larger financial objectives into smaller, manageable steps to facilitate continuous progress.

Seeking support from friends, family, or support groups can provide emotional assistance during challenging times. Sharing experiences and learning from others who have navigated similar situations can be both reassuring and motivating.

In cases of overwhelming debt, seeking legal advice can provide clarity on options such as bankruptcy or debt restructuring. Legal professionals can guide individuals through the legal aspects of resolving financial challenges.

Cultivating a positive mindset is crucial in overcoming the psychological impact of debt. Focusing on progress, learning from financial challenges, and acknowledging achievements, no matter how small, contribute to a more optimistic outlook.

Aligning financial goals with personal values enhances

the sense of purpose and motivation. Recognizing the broader purpose of financial efforts, such as providing for family or pursuing meaningful experiences, adds depth to the financial journey.

Embracing a mindset of continuous learning and adaptability is vital in navigating financial challenges. Staying informed about financial management, seeking new opportunities, and adapting to changing circumstances contribute to resilience and growth.

The psychology of debt is a multifaceted aspect of personal finance that encompasses a wide range of emotions, cognitive processes, and life impacts. Acknowledging the emotional and psychological dimensions of indebtedness is crucial for individuals striving to overcome the challenges associated with debt. By implementing coping strategies, seeking support, and adopting proactive financial practices, individuals can mitigate the psychological impact of debt and work towards financial well-being. Understanding that addressing debt involves both practical and emotional components is a key step in building a healthier relationship with money and fostering a positive financial mindset.

Investing Behavior

Investing behavior is a fascinating and complex field that explores how individuals make decisions, manage risks, and navigate the financial markets when it comes to allocating their resources. The study of investing behavior delves into the psychological, emotional, and cognitive factors that influence the choices individuals make regarding investments. From risk tolerance to market trends, behavioral biases, and decision-making processes, investing behavior is a rich tapestry that shapes the financial landscape for investors. In this exploration, we will delve into various aspects of investing behavior, examining the psychological underpinnings, common behavioral biases, strategies for successful investing, and the impact of emotions on investment decisions.

Risk tolerance is a fundamental aspect of investing behavior that reflects an individual's willingness and ability to withstand fluctuations in the value of their investments. Psychological factors such as personal experiences, financial goals, and individual temperament play a crucial role in determining an investor's risk tolerance. Some individuals may embrace risk as an opportunity for higher returns, while others may be more risk-averse, prioritizing capital preservation.

Investors' time horizons, or the duration they intend to hold investments, are influenced by psychological factors. Long-term investors may be more inclined to weather short-term market fluctuations, focusing on the potential for compound growth over time. In contrast, short-term investors may be more reactive to immediate market conditions, driven by a desire for quick gains or avoiding short-term losses.

Overconfidence is a cognitive bias that can impact

investing behavior. Some investors may exhibit overconfidence in their ability to predict market movements or select winning investments. This bias can lead to excessive trading, disregarding risks, and overestimating one's financial acumen. Overconfident investors may be more susceptible to market volatility.

Loss aversion is a psychological phenomenon wherein individuals feel the pain of losses more acutely than the pleasure of equivalent gains. This bias can influence investment decisions, leading investors to avoid selling losing positions even when it may be rational to do so. Loss aversion can contribute to a reluctance to take necessary actions to rebalance portfolios.

Regret aversion is a behavioral bias driven by the fear of making the wrong decision and experiencing regret. Investors influenced by regret aversion may avoid certain investments or strategies to minimize the possibility of regret. This bias can hinder individuals from taking calculated risks that align with their financial goals.

Herd mentality, or the tendency to follow the crowd, can significantly impact investing behavior. Investors may be influenced by the actions of others, leading to a collective movement in the market. This behavior can contribute to market bubbles, where asset prices become detached from their intrinsic values due to mass participation based on perceived trends.

Confirmation bias is the tendency to seek information that confirms pre-existing beliefs and to avoid information that challenges those beliefs. In investing, confirmation bias can lead individuals to selectively interpret data to support their views, potentially ignoring warning signs or alternative perspectives. This bias can hinder objective analysis and decision-making.

The availability heuristic is a mental shortcut where individuals rely on readily available information, often from recent experiences or memorable events, to make decisions. In investing, this bias can lead to disproportionate reactions based on recent market events, potentially overlooking historical trends or long-term fundamentals.

Anchoring involves relying too heavily on the first piece of information encountered when making decisions. In investing, individuals may anchor their expectations or valuations based on initial market conditions or historical prices. This bias can influence perceptions of value and impact decision-making processes.

FOMO is a powerful emotional driver in investing behavior. The fear of missing out on potential gains can lead investors to make impulsive decisions, follow market trends without thorough analysis, and engage in speculative behavior. FOMO-driven actions may result in suboptimal investment outcomes.

Recency bias involves giving more weight to recent events when making decisions. In investing, this bias can lead individuals to extrapolate recent market trends into the future. Investors influenced by recency bias may overreact to short-term fluctuations without considering broader market dynamics.

The disposition effect refers to the tendency of investors to sell winning investments too early and hold onto losing investments for too long. This behavior is driven by the desire to secure profits and avoid realizing losses, even when rational decision-making suggests a different course of action.

The gambler's fallacy is the belief that past events influence the probability of future outcomes, especially in random processes. In investing, this fallacy may manifest when investors believe that a stock's past performance, whether positive or negative, predicts its future trajectory. This bias can lead to misguided investment decisions.

The sunk cost fallacy involves continuing an investment or decision based on the amount already invested, regardless of the rational analysis of future prospects. Investors influenced by the sunk cost fallacy may hesitate to sell a losing position because they are emotionally attached to recovering past losses.

Optimism bias is the tendency to believe that positive events are more likely to happen than negative ones. In investing, this bias can lead individuals to overestimate the potential for positive outcomes and underestimate risks. Optimism bias may contribute to excessive risk-taking and a lack of preparedness for adverse scenarios.

Investors may exhibit underreaction or overreaction to new information. Underreaction occurs when investors are slow to adjust their views based on new information, while overreaction involves exaggerated responses. Both behaviors can contribute to market inefficiencies and create opportunities for astute investors.

Diversification is a cornerstone of successful investing behavior. Spreading investments across different asset classes helps mitigate risks associated with individual securities or market sectors. Diversified portfolios are better positioned to weather market fluctuations and reduce the impact of specific asset underperformance.

Adopting a long-term perspective is crucial for successful investing. Short-term market fluctuations and volatility are inevitable, but a focus on long-term financial goals allows investors to ride out market cycles and benefit from the power of compounding.

Maintaining discipline in investment decisions involves sticking to a well-thought-out investment plan and avoiding impulsive actions. Disciplined investors resist the urge to make emotional decisions based on short-term market movements and adhere to their predetermined strategies.

The investment landscape is dynamic, and continuous learning is essential for informed decision-making. Keeping abreast of market trends, economic indicators, and financial news enhances an investor's ability to make well-informed choices and adapt to changing market conditions.

Successful investors prioritize risk management. This involves assessing and understanding the risks associated with each investment, implementing risk mitigation strategies, and setting appropriate risk limits. By managing risks effectively, investors can protect their portfolios from significant losses during market downturns.

Attempting to time the market, predicting short-term price movements, is a challenging and often futile endeavor. Successful investors recognize the limitations of market timing and focus on a consistent, long-term investment strategy. Timing the market involves substantial risk and can lead to missed opportunities.

Stress testing involves simulating various adverse scenarios to assess how a portfolio might perform under different conditions. By stress testing portfolios, investors can identify potential weaknesses, make informed adjustments, and ensure that their investments remain resilient in the face of market challenges.

Aligning investments with specific financial goals is a prudent approach. Whether saving for retirement, education, or a major purchase, goal-based investing provides clarity and purpose. Investors can tailor their strategies to meet the specific time horizon and risk tolerance associated with each financial objective.

Regularly rebalancing a portfolio involves adjusting asset allocations to maintain the desired risk-return profile. Market movements can lead to deviations from the original allocation, and rebalancing ensures that the portfolio stays in line with the investor's long-term objectives.

Emotional regulation is essential for successful investing behavior. Emotions such as fear, greed, and panic can lead to irrational decisions. Investors who develop emotional resilience and the ability to stay calm during market fluctuations are better positioned to make rational choices and avoid impulsive actions.

Markets evolve, and economic conditions change. Successful investors regularly evaluate their investment strategies in light of evolving circumstances. This may involve reassessing financial goals, adjusting risk tolerance, and incorporating new information into investment decisions.

Dollar-cost averaging is a systematic investment approach where investors contribute a fixed amount at regular intervals, regardless of market conditions. This strategy helps smooth out the impact of market volatility, as investors buy more shares when prices are low and fewer shares when prices are high.

Thorough research and due diligence are critical components of successful investing behavior. Before making investment decisions, investors should conduct in-depth research on potential assets, assess their financial health, and consider factors such as management quality and industry trends.

Successful investors demonstrate adaptability to changing market conditions. This may involve adjusting asset allocations, exploring new investment opportunities, or reallocating resources based on evolving economic trends. Adaptability is key to navigating the dynamic nature of financial markets.

The role of emotions in investment decisions is profound and can significantly influence outcomes. Several emotions can impact investment behavior, including:

Fear can lead to conservative investment choices or even prompt investors to exit the market during periods of uncertainty. Fear-driven decisions may result in missed opportunities for growth or recovery.

Greed can drive investors to take excessive risks in pursuit of high returns. This may lead to speculative behavior, overleveraging, and exposure to significant losses.

Panic-induced decisions can result in abrupt selling during market downturns, often at the bottom of the cycle. Panic selling can crystallize losses and hinder the potential for recovery.

Overconfidence can lead to excessive trading, overestimation of one's ability to predict market movements, and a reluctance to acknowledge the potential for losses.

Regret over past investment decisions, whether gains or losses, can influence future choices. Investors may avoid certain actions to prevent experiencing regret, even if those actions are rational.

Excitement can lead to impulsive decisions driven by the thrill of potential gains. This emotional high may cloud rational judgment and contribute to risk-taking behavior.

Hopeful optimism may lead investors to hold onto underperforming assets in the anticipation of a future recovery. While optimism is valuable, it should be balanced with realistic assessments of market conditions.

Understanding the impact of emotions on investment decisions is crucial for investors seeking to enhance their decision-making processes. Developing emotional intelligence, practicing mindfulness, and incorporating strategies to manage emotional responses contribute to more rational and objective investment behavior.

Investing behavior is a multifaceted interplay of psychological, emotional, and cognitive factors that significantly influence how individuals navigate the complex world of financial markets. Recognizing and understanding these factors is essential for investors seeking to make informed decisions, manage risks, and achieve their financial goals.

Successful investing behavior involves a combination of disciplined strategies, risk management practices, and emotional intelligence. Investors who adopt a long-term perspective, remain adaptable to changing market conditions, and continuously evaluate their investment strategies are better positioned for financial success.

By acknowledging common behavioral biases, employing prudent investment strategies, and cultivating emotional resilience, investors can navigate the challenges of investing behavior and build a robust foundation for their financial future. Ultimately, a balanced and informed approach to investing behavior contributes to the achievement of long-term financial objectives and overall financial well-being.

Ethical and Sustainable Investing

In recent years, there has been a notable shift in the world of finance as investors increasingly seek avenues that align with their ethical and sustainable values. This movement goes beyond traditional financial metrics, incorporating environmental, social, and governance (ESG) factors into investment decisions. Ethical and sustainable investing, often referred to as socially responsible investing (SRI) or impact investing, reflects a conscious effort to contribute to positive social and environmental outcomes while generating financial returns. In this exploration, we delve into the principles, strategies, challenges, and impact of ethical and sustainable investing.

Ethical and sustainable investing involves making investment decisions based on both financial considerations and ethical or sustainable principles. Investors seek to support companies and industries that align with their values, fostering positive social and environmental impact alongside financial returns. This approach acknowledges the interconnectedness of financial markets with broader societal and environmental challenges.

ESG criteria serve as a framework for evaluating the ethical and sustainable performance of companies. These criteria encompass a range of factors, including environmental impact (E), social responsibility (S), and corporate governance (G). Investors use ESG considerations to assess how companies manage risks, address societal issues, and uphold ethical standards.

Ethical and sustainable investors employ screening processes to select or exclude specific investments based on predefined criteria. Positive screening involves selecting companies that exhibit positive ESG attributes, such as those with strong environmental practices or commitment to social responsibility. Negative screening excludes investments in industries or companies that engage in activities contrary to ethical or sustainable principles, such as tobacco or weapons manufacturing.

Impact investing takes ethical and sustainable investing a step further by explicitly seeking measurable positive social or environmental impact alongside financial returns. Impact investors actively contribute to solutions for global challenges, such as climate change, poverty alleviation, or healthcare accessibility. Impact investments aim to generate a tangible and beneficial outcome beyond financial gains.

The roots of ethical investing can be traced back to religious groups and individuals who sought to align their investment choices with moral and ethical values. In the modern context, ethical investing gained momentum in the latter half of the 20th century as social and environmental awareness grew. The 21st century has witnessed a significant acceleration of interest in sustainable finance, driven by a broader recognition of the impact of business activities on the planet and society.

Ethical and sustainable investing has transitioned from a niche approach to an increasingly mainstream investment strategy. As awareness of ESG factors has risen, institutional investors, asset managers, and even large corporations are integrating ethical considerations into their investment processes. This shift reflects a broader acknowledgment of the importance of sustainability in long-term financial success.

The development of global standards and reporting frameworks has played a pivotal role in advancing ethical and sustainable investing. Organizations like the Global Reporting Initiative (GRI) and the Sustainability Accounting Standards

Board (SASB) provide guidelines for companies to disclose their ESG performance, facilitating more transparent and standardized reporting.

Regulatory bodies in various jurisdictions have started recognizing the significance of ethical and sustainable investing. Some countries mandate or encourage companies to disclose ESG information. Additionally, regulatory support is growing for investment products that adhere to ESG principles, reinforcing the legitimacy and importance of ethical considerations in the investment landscape.

Ethical and sustainable investors often prioritize companies with a strong commitment to environmental stewardship. This may include a focus on reducing carbon emissions, transitioning to renewable energy sources, minimizing environmental pollution, and adopting sustainable resource management practices.

Social responsibility is a core principle of ethical investing, emphasizing the positive contributions companies make to society. This can encompass fair labor practices, diversity and inclusion initiatives, community engagement, and support for human rights. Investors seek to align with companies that prioritize the well-being of their employees, communities, and broader societal impact.

The governance practices of a company play a crucial role in ethical and sustainable investing. Investors assess factors such as board diversity, executive compensation structures, shareholder rights, and overall corporate transparency. Strong corporate governance is seen as indicative of a company's commitment to ethical conduct and responsible decision-making.

Ethical and sustainable investing is often aligned with a long-term view of value creation. Investors recognize that companies focused on sustainable practices are better positioned to navigate future challenges, including regulatory changes, societal shifts, and environmental risks. Prioritizing long-term value over short-term gains is a key tenet of ethical investing.

Thematic investing involves targeting specific themes or sectors aligned with ethical and sustainable principles. Examples include investing in clean energy, water conservation, or healthcare innovation. Thematic investments allow investors to align their portfolios with causes they are passionate about.

ESG integration involves incorporating ESG factors into traditional financial analysis. This approach acknowledges that ESG considerations can impact a company's financial performance and risk profile. Investors assess how well companies manage ESG risks and opportunities alongside traditional financial metrics.

Impact bonds and financing mechanisms provide capital to projects with measurable social or environmental outcomes. Social impact bonds, for instance, involve private investors financing social programs, with returns tied to the program's success in achieving predefined outcomes. This strategy directly links financial returns with positive societal impact.

Negative screening remains a common strategy in ethical and sustainable investing. Investors exclude certain industries or companies from their portfolios based on ethical considerations. Common exclusions include companies involved in tobacco, firearms, fossil fuels, or other activities deemed incompatible with ethical principles.

One challenge in ethical and sustainable investing is the lack of a universally agreed-upon definition of what constitutes ethical or sustainable. Different investors may prioritize different criteria, leading to variations in approaches and potential ambiguity in assessing the impact of investments.

Greenwashing refers to the practice of companies presenting themselves as more environmentally friendly or socially responsible than they actually are. Investors face the challenge of discerning genuine commitment to ethical principles from marketing strategies designed to capitalize on the growing demand for sustainable investments.

Critics argue that prioritizing ethical and sustainable considerations may result in trade-offs with financial returns. Some contend that limiting investment choices based on ESG criteria may lead to missed opportunities for financial gains, potentially impacting portfolio performance.

Measuring the impact of ethical and sustainable investments poses a complex challenge. While financial returns can be quantified, assessing the societal or environmental impact of an investment is inherently subjective and may lack standardized measurement metrics. Investors and stakeholders are increasingly calling for more standardized impact measurement methodologies to ensure transparency and accountability.

The absence of consistent and universally applied regulations in the ethical and sustainable investing space can create challenges. Varying regulatory frameworks across jurisdictions make it difficult for investors to navigate and may result in inconsistencies in disclosure requirements and reporting standards.

Ethical and sustainable investing often focuses on larger, more established companies with robust reporting practices. Small and mid-cap companies, which may lack the resources for extensive reporting, can be overlooked. This limitation may restrict the scope of ethical investing and exclude innovative, sustainable ventures in their early stages.

Analyzing ESG data can be complex due to the sheer volume of information and the subjective nature of some criteria. Investors may face challenges in comparing ESG performance across companies and industries, hindering the ability to make informed investment decisions based on comprehensive and standardized data.

Ethical and sustainable investing has demonstrated its potential to influence corporate behavior positively. Companies aware of investor expectations regarding ESG performance may adjust their practices to align with ethical principles, contributing to positive societal and environmental outcomes.

The demand for ethical and sustainable investments has encouraged industries to transition toward more sustainable practices. Sectors such as renewable energy, green technology, and sustainable agriculture have witnessed increased investment, fostering innovation and promoting environmentally conscious solutions.

Ethical and sustainable investing has driven a push for greater transparency and disclosure regarding ESG practices. Companies are increasingly recognizing the importance of communicating their ethical and sustainable initiatives to meet investor expectations and comply with evolving reporting standards.

The focus on ESG considerations in investing has played a role in raising awareness of environmental, social, and governance issues. Investors, companies, and the public are more informed about the impact of business activities on broader societal and environmental challenges, fostering a collective effort toward positive change.

Ethical and sustainable investing in equities involves selecting stocks based on ESG criteria. Investors may opt for companies demonstrating strong ethical practices, sustainable business models, and a commitment to positive societal impact. Ethical equity funds and indices have gained popularity to facilitate diversified exposure to such stocks.

Ethical considerations extend to fixed-income investments, where investors may seek bonds issued by entities aligned with ethical and sustainable principles. Green bonds, social impact bonds, and sustainability-linked bonds are examples of fixed-income instruments designed to support environmentally or socially responsible projects.

Ethical and sustainable investing in real estate involves considering ESG factors in property selection and management. Investors may focus on environmentally friendly buildings, energy-efficient features, and social impact initiatives within communities. Sustainable real estate investment trusts (REITs) cater to those seeking ethical exposure in the real estate sector.

Ethical investing extends to venture capital and private equity, where investors support startups and private companies aligned with ethical and sustainable principles. Impact-focused venture capital funds seek investments that deliver both financial returns and positive societal impact, contributing to the growth of sustainable businesses.

The integration of artificial intelligence (AI) is anticipated to play a significant role in advancing ethical and sustainable investing. AI algorithms can analyze vast amounts of ESG data, identify patterns, and assess the impact of companies' sustainability practices with greater efficiency, contributing to more informed investment decisions.

Blockchain technology holds promise in enhancing transparency and traceability in ethical and sustainable investing. The decentralized nature of blockchain ensures immutable records, reducing the risk of greenwashing and providing investors with verifiable information about a company's ethical and sustainable practices.

The industry is likely to witness ongoing innovations in impact measurement methodologies. The development of standardized metrics and frameworks for assessing the societal and environmental impact of investments will address current challenges and provide investors with clearer insights into the outcomes of their ethical and sustainable portfolios.

The growing demand for ethical and sustainable investments is expected to lead to an expansion of ESG offerings across asset classes. Financial institutions, asset managers, and investment platforms are likely to introduce a broader range of investment products that cater to diverse ethical preferences and sustainability goals.

Ethical and sustainable investing represents a transformative force in the financial landscape, challenging traditional paradigms by emphasizing the integration of ethical principles and sustainability considerations into investment decisions. The movement towards aligning investments with values reflects a broader societal shift towards responsible and conscientious capitalism.

While ethical and sustainable investing has made significant strides, challenges such as definitional ambiguity, greenwashing, and the need for standardized impact measurement persist. The industry's future evolution will likely be shaped by technological advancements, increased regulatory support, and a continued focus on transparency and accountability.

As investors increasingly recognize the interconnectedness of financial success with environmental and social well-being, ethical and sustainable investing is poised to play a pivotal role in shaping a more conscientious and sustainable global economy. The continued growth of this movement holds the potential to drive positive change, encouraging businesses to adopt responsible practices and contributing to a more sustainable and equitable future.

Money and Relationships

oney and relationships are deeply interconnected aspects of our lives, shaping the dynamics, communication, and overall well-being of individuals and couples. The intersection of money and relationships involves shared financial goals, communication about finances, individual money mindsets, and the potential for both positive collaboration and challenges. In this exploration, we delve into the multifaceted relationship between money and relationships, examining how financial matters impact partnerships, strategies for effective communication, common financial challenges, and ways to cultivate financial harmony within relationships.

Shared financial goals provide a foundation for couples to align their aspirations and work collaboratively towards a common future. Whether saving for a home, planning for children's education, or building a retirement fund, having shared financial objectives fosters unity and purpose in a relationship.

Open and transparent communication about finances is a cornerstone of healthy relationships. Discussing income, expenses, budgeting, and long-term financial plans creates a shared understanding of the financial landscape. Regular financial check-ins can strengthen the partnership and promote a sense of joint responsibility.

Individuals often bring distinct money mindsets shaped by their upbringing, experiences, and values. Understanding and respecting these differences is crucial in navigating financial decisions. Whether one partner is more risk-averse or the other is inclined towards spending, recognizing and discussing individual money mindsets contributes to mutual understanding.

Achieving a balance between financial independence and interdependence is key in relationships. While financial independence allows individuals to maintain autonomy, interdependence involves collaborative decision-making and shared responsibilities. Striking the right balance ensures that both partners contribute to and benefit from the financial aspects of the relationship.

Money serves as a tool for making lifestyle choices within a relationship. From travel and leisure activities to major life decisions, the availability and allocation of financial resources impact the lifestyle a couple can afford. Negotiating and aligning lifestyle choices contribute to a sense of fulfillment and satisfaction in the relationship.

Transparency is foundational in financial communication. Both partners should openly share details about income, expenses, debts, and financial goals. Creating an environment where financial discussions are free from judgment encourages trust and facilitates effective communication.

Collaboratively setting financial goals ensures that both partners have a say in shaping the financial future of the relationship. Whether short-term or long-term, goal-setting fosters a sense of shared purpose and motivates joint efforts to achieve those objectives.

Developing a budget together is a practical step in managing finances. A joint budget outlines income, expenses, savings, and discretionary spending. Regularly revisiting and adjusting the budget based on changing circumstances promotes ongoing financial alignment.

Building and maintaining an emergency fund is a shared responsibility that provides a financial safety net for unexpected expenses. Agreeing on the purpose and target amount for an emergency fund ensures preparedness and reduces financial stress during unforeseen challenges.

Clearly defining financial roles and responsibilities helps distribute the workload and avoids misunderstandings. Whether one partner manages bills while the other focuses on investments, having clarity about financial roles ensures efficient financial management.

Recognizing and addressing differences in money mindsets requires open communication and empathy. Discussing financial priorities, values, and long-term visions helps bridge gaps and find common ground in financial decision-making.

Regular financial check-ins provide dedicated time for discussing financial matters. These check-ins may involve reviewing the budget, tracking progress towards financial goals, and addressing any concerns or changes in circumstances.

Conflicts about money are inevitable in relationships, but handling them constructively is crucial. Instead of placing blame, focus on understanding each other's perspectives, finding compromises, and seeking solutions that align with both partners' values and priorities.

Income disparities between partners can pose challenges, especially if not addressed openly. Unequal earning potential may require intentional discussions about how to manage finances, contribute to shared goals, and maintain a sense of financial equality.

Disagreements about debt management can arise when one partner has significant debts or a different attitude towards borrowing. Transparent discussions about existing debts, future borrowing plans, and strategies for debt repayment are essential for financial harmony.

Differences in spending habits, such as one partner being

a spender while the other is a saver, can lead to conflicts. Establishing spending boundaries, setting discretionary spending limits, and finding compromises can help navigate divergent spending habits.

Hidden financial issues, such as undisclosed debts or secret spending, erode trust within a relationship. Creating an environment of financial transparency and honesty is crucial for addressing and preventing hidden financial issues.

Unplanned financial events, such as job loss, medical emergencies, or unexpected expenses, can strain relationships. Having contingency plans, emergency funds, and open communication about how to handle such events helps couples navigate unforeseen challenges.

Conflicting financial priorities may arise when partners have different visions for the use of money. Addressing these conflicts involves finding common ground, prioritizing shared goals, and making compromises to ensure that both partners' needs and aspirations are considered.

External influences, such as family expectations or societal pressure, can impact financial decisions within a relationship. Couples may need to navigate external expectations while maintaining autonomy in their financial choices and priorities.

Trust is fundamental in financial relationships. Building and maintaining trust involves being transparent about financial matters, honoring commitments, and working collaboratively towards shared goals.

Joint financial education enhances the ability of both partners to make informed decisions. Attend financial workshops, read books, or take courses together to deepen your understanding of personal finance and investment strategies.

Clearly defining shared values and priorities helps guide financial decisions. Whether it's saving for a home, prioritizing education, or planning for retirement, aligning values ensures that financial choices reflect the couple's overarching vision.

Celebrating financial milestones, whether big or small, reinforces positive financial behavior. Acknowledge achievements, such as reaching savings goals or successfully managing debt, to encourage continued collaboration and motivation.

Joint financial goals provide a sense of purpose and collaboration. Establish short-term and long-term goals that reflect both partners' aspirations, ensuring that the financial journey is a shared adventure.

Financial circumstances can change over time, and practicing flexibility and adaptability is crucial in maintaining financial harmony. Be open to reassessing goals, adjusting strategies, and accommodating changes in income or expenses. Flexibility allows couples to navigate unexpected challenges with resilience.

Building emergency funds and creating contingency plans provide a financial safety net. Having resources set aside for unexpected events, coupled with plans on how to handle such situations, reduces stress and enhances the couple's ability to weather financial storms.

Allocating personal spending allowances within the budget allows each partner to have discretionary funds for personal preferences without affecting shared financial goals. This approach recognizes individual autonomy while maintaining financial responsibility.

Seeking professional financial guidance, such as consulting a financial advisor or planner, can offer objective insights and strategies tailored to the couple's unique situation. Professional advice can enhance financial literacy and assist in making informed decisions.

Financial plans should be dynamic and subject to regular

review and adjustment. Life circumstances, financial goals, and external factors may change, necessitating updates to the financial plan. Regular reviews ensure that the couple's financial strategies remain relevant and effective.

Cultivating a team mentality in financial matters reinforces the idea that both partners are working together towards shared objectives. Approach financial challenges and decisions as a team, acknowledging that collaboration strengthens the relationship and enhances financial outcomes.

Maintaining a positive financial mindset contributes to a healthier relationship with money. Emphasize the opportunities for growth, learning, and shared achievements rather than dwelling solely on challenges. A positive outlook fosters resilience in the face of financial ups and downs.

Expressing gratitude for each other's financial contributions, whether through income, budgeting efforts, or shared responsibilities, reinforces appreciation and acknowledgment. Regular expressions of gratitude contribute to a positive and supportive financial environment.

Establishing financial rituals, such as regular budget meetings or joint financial planning sessions, creates a structured and consistent approach to managing finances. These rituals provide dedicated time for discussing financial matters and reinforce the importance of collaboration.

In the early stages of a relationship, financial dynamics may center around shared activities, dating expenses, and individual financial habits. Open communication about financial expectations, such as who pays for what, sets the foundation for healthy financial discussions.

As couples move in together or get married, the financial aspects become more intertwined. Discussions about joint bank accounts, shared expenses, and long-term financial goals become pivotal. Creating a joint budget and clearly defining financial responsibilities helps establish a solid financial partnership.

Parenthood introduces new financial considerations, from childcare expenses to education planning. Couples navigate decisions about parental leave, childcare arrangements, and the allocation of financial resources to support the well-being and future of their family.

The empty nest phase, when children leave home, and retirement bring new financial dynamics. Couples may reassess their financial goals, plan for retirement, and make decisions about downsizing or relocating. Adjusting to changes in income and expenses becomes crucial during these stages.

In later life, couples engage in legacy planning, considering how to pass on assets, manage healthcare costs, and plan for the later stages of retirement. Legal considerations, such as wills and estate planning, become significant aspects of the financial conversation.

Communication is the bedrock of overcoming financial challenges. Openly discuss financial concerns, share perspectives, and actively listen to each other's viewpoints. Creating a safe space for honest communication fosters understanding and collaboration.

If financial challenges persist or become overwhelming, seeking professional help is a proactive step. Financial advisors, counselors, or therapists with expertise in financial matters can offer guidance and strategies to address specific challenges.

Approach financial challenges as a team, engaging in collaborative problem-solving. Brainstorming solutions, setting mutual goals, and working together to implement strategies contribute to a sense of shared responsibility and accomplishment.

Invest in financial education as a couple. Attend workshops, read books, or enroll in courses that enhance your understanding of personal finance. Shared financial literacy deepens the couple's knowledge and empowers informed decision-making.

Realistic expectations are crucial in navigating financial challenges. Understand that financial ups and downs are a natural part of life. Setting realistic expectations prepares couples to face challenges with resilience and a constructive mindset.

Cultivate empathy and understanding for each other's perspectives and experiences. Recognize that individuals may have different approaches to money based on their upbringing, values, and personal experiences. Empathy promotes a supportive environment for addressing financial challenges.

Prioritize emotional well-being alongside financial solutions. Financial challenges can be emotionally taxing, and addressing the emotional aspects is essential for overall relationship health. Be supportive, acknowledge emotions, and seek positive coping mechanisms.

Celebrate small wins and milestones along the way. Acknowledge progress, no matter how incremental, to reinforce positive financial behavior. Celebrating achievements together fosters a sense of accomplishment and motivation.

In conclusion, the relationship between money and relationships is intricate and dynamic, influencing various aspects of individuals' lives at different stages of their journey together. Financial harmony in relationships is not solely about the numbers; it encompasses open communication, shared goals, and a commitment to navigating challenges together.

Couples who actively engage in conversations about money, set joint financial goals, and approach financial challenges collaboratively are better positioned to build a resilient and harmonious financial partnership. Embracing a mindset of continuous learning, adaptability, and mutual support contributes to a positive financial environment and strengthens the foundation of the relationship.

It is crucial to recognize that each relationship is unique, and there is no one-size-fits-all approach to managing finances. The key lies in understanding and respecting each other's perspectives, aligning financial values, and finding customized strategies that work for the specific dynamics of the partnership.

As couples navigate the complexities of money and relationships, they have the opportunity to not only build a secure financial future but also deepen their connection and understanding of each other. The journey involves ongoing communication, shared decision-making, and a commitment to growing together through the various stages of life.

By cultivating financial transparency, setting realistic expectations, and prioritizing emotional well-being, couples can overcome challenges, celebrate achievements, and create a fulfilling and sustainable financial partnership. Ultimately, the journey of managing money within relationships is a shared adventure that contributes to the overall health, happiness, and longevity of the partnership.

Consumerism and Happiness

onsumerism and happiness represent two intertwined concepts that have become central to modern societies. Consumerism, characterized by the continuous pursuit of material goods and services, plays a significant role in shaping economies and cultures worldwide. On the other hand, happiness, a subjective and multifaceted emotional state, is a fundamental aspect of human well-being. This exploration delves into the relationship between consumerism and happiness, examining the impact of consumer culture on individuals and societies, the pursuit of material possessions as a source of happiness, and alternative paths to a more meaningful and sustainable sense of fulfillment.

Consumerism is a socio-economic and cultural phenomenon characterized by the constant acquisition and consumption of goods and services. Rooted in the industrial revolution, consumerism gained momentum in the 20th century with the rise of mass production, advertising, and a shift towards a market-driven economy. Today, consumerism is deeply ingrained in societies globally, shaping lifestyles, values, and societal norms.

Materialism, a core component of consumerism, involves placing a high value on material possessions and their acquisition as a means of achieving happiness and success. The pursuit of possessions becomes a driving force, with individuals seeking fulfillment through the accumulation of wealth, luxury items, and the latest products.

Advertising plays a pivotal role in fueling consumerism by creating desires and shaping preferences. Through sophisticated marketing strategies, individuals are persuaded to associate happiness, status, and identity with specific products. The influence of advertising extends beyond tangible goods, encompassing experiences, lifestyles, and societal expectations.

Consumerism contributes to a disposable culture where products are rapidly consumed and discarded. The rise of fast fashion, planned obsolescence in technology, and single-use items contribute to environmental degradation and resource depletion. The ecological footprint of consumerism raises concerns about sustainability and the long-term well-being of the planet.

The pursuit of consumerist ideals often leads individuals into debt as they strive to maintain a certain lifestyle or acquire desired possessions. Financial stress resulting from excessive debt can have detrimental effects on mental health, relationships, and overall life satisfaction.

The hedonic treadmill is a psychological concept suggesting that individuals adapt to changes in their circumstances, returning to a baseline level of happiness despite positive or negative life events. In the context of consumerism, the pursuit of possessions and wealth may provide temporary boosts in happiness, but individuals often find themselves on a perpetual treadmill, constantly seeking the next acquisition for sustained satisfaction.

Consumerism often promotes instant gratification, offering quick and easily attainable pleasures through the purchase of goods and experiences. However, the joy derived from these acquisitions is often short-lived, leading to a cycle of continuous consumption in the quest for sustained happiness.

Consumerism fuels social comparison, with individuals measuring their success and happiness against others based on material possessions. The pursuit of status through conspicuous consumption becomes a driving force, as individuals seek external validation and a sense of achievement through the display of wealth and possessions.

Social media amplifies the impact of consumerism by creating platforms for individuals to showcase their lifestyles and possessions. The curated portrayal of an idealized life on social media platforms can intensify the desire for material success, contributing to a culture of comparison and competition.

Lifestyle brands leverage consumer aspirations by marketing not only products but also a desirable way of life. The association of a brand with a particular lifestyle creates a sense of identity for consumers, leading them to believe that adopting the brand's products will bring them closer to the envisioned lifestyle and, consequently, happiness.

Research suggests that experiences tend to contribute more significantly to long-term happiness than material possessions. Engaging in meaningful experiences, building relationships, and creating lasting memories offer a more enduring source of fulfillment compared to the transient joy derived from possessions.

Shifting towards values-based living involves aligning one's actions and choices with personal values and principles. Rather than focusing on external markers of success dictated by consumer culture, individuals find deeper satisfaction by pursuing a life in harmony with their intrinsic values.

Mindfulness, the practice of being present and fully engaged in the current moment, offers an alternative to the constant pursuit of future desires. Cultivating mindfulness allows individuals to appreciate and find contentment in the present, reducing the need for external stimuli to attain happiness.

Strong social connections and a sense of community have a profound impact on happiness. Investing time in building and nurturing relationships, contributing to the well-being of others, and fostering a sense of belonging provide a sustainable foundation for happiness beyond material pursuits.

Investing in personal development and continuous growth contributes to a sense of purpose and fulfillment. Pursuing education, acquiring new skills, and setting personal goals that align with one's passions foster a deeper and more enduring form of happiness.

Embracing environmental consciousness involves making choices that consider the ecological impact of consumer behavior. Sustainable living, responsible consumption, and a commitment to reducing one's carbon footprint contribute to a more conscientious and sustainable approach to happiness.

Practicing gratitude and adopting principles of positive psychology can shift the focus from what is lacking to appreciating what is present. Regularly expressing gratitude, cultivating a positive mindset, and fostering a sense of optimism contribute to an overall sense of well-being.

Conscious consumption involves making deliberate and informed choices about what to buy and consume. Individuals can adopt a more mindful approach by considering the environmental impact, ethical considerations, and the long-term value of their purchases.

Minimalism advocates for simplifying one's life by decluttering possessions and focusing on essential and meaningful items. Embracing minimalism encourages individuals to question the necessity of material possessions and prioritize experiences and relationships over excess belongings.

Financial literacy empowers individuals to make informed decisions about money, budgeting, and investing. Responsible spending involves aligning expenses with financial goals, avoiding unnecessary debt, and making choices that contribute to long-term financial well-being.

Breaking the cycle of consumerism involves educating future generations about alternative paths to happiness.

Teaching values of sustainability, mindfulness, and conscious consumption equips individuals with the tools to make choices that prioritize well-being over materialism.

Advocating for systemic change involves addressing the structural issues that perpetuate consumerism and its negative impacts on both individuals and the environment. This may include supporting policies that promote sustainability, ethical production practices, and responsible marketing. By actively participating in efforts to reshape societal norms and consumer behaviors, individuals can contribute to a broader shift towards a more balanced and mindful approach to consumption.

Shifting towards a holistic well-being model involves recognizing that happiness is multifaceted and extends beyond material possessions. Individuals can develop a personalized well-being model that considers physical health, mental well-being, social connections, and a sense of purpose, integrating these elements for a more comprehensive and sustainable source of happiness.

Developing media literacy skills is crucial in navigating the pervasive influence of advertising and consumer culture. Being aware of the persuasive techniques used in marketing allows individuals to critically evaluate messages and make conscious decisions about the products and lifestyles they choose to embrace.

Actively engaging with the community fosters a sense of connection and shared purpose. Participating in local initiatives, volunteering, and collaborating with others to address common challenges provide a sense of fulfillment that goes beyond individual pursuits and contributes to collective well-being.

The rise of technology has facilitated consumerism through online shopping, social media influence, and constant exposure to advertising. Cultivating a healthy relationship with technology involves setting boundaries, practicing digital mindfulness, and leveraging technology for positive connections and personal growth rather than as a tool for endless consumption.

Encouraging cultural shifts towards a more balanced and sustainable perspective on happiness requires collective efforts. Communities, educational institutions, and influencers can play a role in promoting values that prioritize well-being, environmental responsibility, and meaningful connections over excessive materialism.

Governments can implement policies that encourage responsible consumption and environmental sustainability. This may include regulations on advertising, incentives for eco-friendly practices, and initiatives to promote ethical production and fair labor practices.

Incorporating financial education into educational curricula equips individuals with the knowledge and skills needed to make informed financial decisions. Governments and educational institutions can collaborate to develop programs that empower individuals to manage their finances responsibly.

Governments play a crucial role in environmental conservation by implementing policies that address climate change, resource depletion, and pollution. By promoting sustainable practices and incentivizing businesses to adopt eco-friendly measures, governments contribute to a more sustainable and responsible approach to consumption.

Governments can support local and sustainable businesses through initiatives such as grants, tax incentives, and certification programs. By promoting businesses that adhere to ethical and environmentally friendly practices, governments contribute to a shift in consumer preferences towards responsible and conscious consumption.

Public awareness campaigns led by governments can educate the population about the impact of consumerism on well-being and the environment. These campaigns can promote alternative paths to happiness, emphasize the importance of sustainable choices, and encourage responsible consumption habits.

Governments can invest in research and development of green technologies that promote sustainability. This includes supporting innovations in renewable energy, waste reduction, and eco-friendly production methods to create a more sustainable foundation for economic growth.

The concept of "enough" embodies a profound shift in perspective, urging individuals to reassess their relationship with material possessions and acknowledge a point where sufficiency and contentment intersect. It transcends the relentless pursuit of excess and prompts a mindful consideration of what truly brings fulfillment. Embracing the idea of "enough" involves recognizing that happiness and well-being extend beyond the accumulation of possessions, urging individuals to find value in experiences, relationships, and personal growth. It signifies a departure from the insatiable desire for more and invites a contented acknowledgment of having reached a satisfactory and sustainable state in various aspects of life, fostering a sense of gratitude for what is present rather than a perpetual quest for what is lacking.

The relationship between consumerism and happiness is complex and multifaceted. While consumerism, driven by the pursuit of material possessions, can provide momentary satisfaction and contribute to economic growth, its negative impacts on well-being and the environment are undeniable. The challenge lies in finding a balance that allows for responsible consumption while prioritizing holistic well-being and environmental sustainability.

Individuals, communities, governments, and institutions all play crucial roles in shaping this relationship. By fostering awareness, promoting values that prioritize well-being over excessive materialism, and advocating for systemic changes, it is possible to navigate towards a more sustainable and balanced coexistence with consumer culture.

In essence, the pursuit of happiness need not be synonymous with endless consumption. True and lasting happiness may lie in meaningful experiences, strong social connections, personal growth, and a conscientious approach to the choices we make in our daily lives. It is a collective journey towards a more mindful and sustainable relationship with the world around us, where happiness is not merely found in what we possess but in how we live and contribute to the well-being of ourselves, others, and the planet.

Financial Education and Literacy

Financial education and literacy play pivotal roles in empowering individuals to make informed and effective financial decisions, thereby influencing their overall well-being and contributing to the economic health of societies. In this comprehensive exploration, we delve into the significance of financial education, the impact of financial literacy on individuals and communities, existing challenges, and strategies to enhance financial education on personal, institutional, and societal levels.

Financial education empowers individuals by providing them with the knowledge and skills needed to navigate the complexities of personal finance. From budgeting and saving to understanding investment options and managing debt, a well-rounded financial education equips individuals to make informed decisions that align with their financial goals.

Financial education instills confidence in individuals to take control of their financial futures. When people understand financial concepts and have the skills to apply them, they are more likely to approach financial challenges with confidence and make decisions that positively impact their economic well-being.

Informed decision-making is a core benefit of financial literacy. Individuals equipped with financial knowledge can make sound choices about spending, saving, investing, and planning for the future. This leads to better financial outcomes, reduced stress, and increased resilience in the face of economic uncertainties.

On a broader scale, financial education contributes to

economic stability. A population with a high level of financial literacy is better equipped to manage personal finances responsibly, reducing the likelihood of financial crises and promoting overall economic resilience.

Financial education helps individuals set and achieve long-term financial goals. Whether it's saving for education, homeownership, or retirement, understanding the principles of financial planning allows individuals to create realistic and achievable goals, setting the stage for financial success over the years.

Financial education can play a role in addressing wealth inequality by providing individuals from diverse backgrounds with the tools to build and grow their financial assets. It serves as a means to level the playing field, offering opportunities for economic advancement and reducing disparities in financial well-being.

Financial literacy directly correlates with improved money management skills. Individuals who are financially literate are better equipped to create budgets, track expenses, and optimize their financial resources, leading to more efficient and responsible money management.

Financial literacy is instrumental in promoting responsible credit use. Understanding the implications of credit scores, interest rates, and debt management allows individuals to use credit wisely, avoid unnecessary debt, and maintain a healthy financial profile.

Financially literate individuals are more likely to prioritize savings and investments. They understand the importance of building emergency funds, contributing to retirement accounts, and exploring investment opportunities to grow their wealth over time.

Retirement planning is a complex aspect of personal finance, and financial literacy plays a crucial role in ensuring individuals make informed decisions about their retirement savings. This includes understanding retirement accounts, investment options, and strategies for income generation in retirement.

Financial literacy is essential for entrepreneurial success. Individuals with an understanding of financial concepts are better positioned to start and manage businesses, make strategic financial decisions, and navigate the financial challenges that entrepreneurs often encounter.

Financial literacy contributes to reduced financial stress. Individuals who are well-versed in financial matters are less likely to feel overwhelmed by money-related concerns, leading to improved mental health and overall well-being.

Financially literate individuals are more adept at recognizing and protecting themselves against financial scams and fraud. Understanding common tactics used by scammers and having knowledge about secure financial practices enhances financial security.

One of the primary challenges in financial education is limited access to quality resources. Disparities in educational opportunities, both geographically and socioeconomically, can result in unequal access to comprehensive financial education.

Financial education is not consistently integrated into school curricula worldwide. The lack of a standardized approach to including financial literacy in educational programs leaves many individuals without the foundational knowledge needed for sound financial decision-making.

Financial systems are often complex, with a myriad of products, services, and investment options. Understanding these complexities requires a certain level of financial literacy that individuals may struggle to attain without proper guidance and education.

Cultural and linguistic barriers can hinder the

effectiveness of financial education initiatives. Tailoring programs to diverse cultural contexts and ensuring that educational materials are accessible in multiple languages is essential to reaching a broader audience.

Financial landscapes evolve, and ongoing education is crucial for individuals to stay informed about changes in financial markets, regulations, and investment opportunities. The lack of easily accessible continuing education programs can leave individuals unaware of important developments.

Motivating individuals to actively engage in financial education can be challenging. Financial topics may be perceived as dry or intimidating, leading to low motivation to seek out and absorb financial knowledge.

A fundamental strategy is the integration of financial education into school curricula at various educational levels. By incorporating age-appropriate financial concepts into subjects like mathematics and social studies, students can develop financial literacy skills early on.

Promoting a culture of lifelong learning encourages individuals to continue educating themselves about financial matters beyond formal education. Online courses, workshops, and seminars can serve as valuable resources for ongoing financial education.

Public awareness campaigns play a crucial role in highlighting the importance of financial literacy. Governments, financial institutions, and nonprofit organizations can collaborate to promote the benefits of financial education and inform individuals about available resources.

Community-based programs offer localized and culturally relevant financial education. These programs can be tailored to address specific challenges and opportunities within communities, fostering a sense of shared responsibility for financial well-being.

Leveraging technology and digital platforms provides accessible and flexible avenues for financial education. Mobile apps, online courses, and interactive platforms offer individuals the opportunity to learn at their own pace and convenience.

Employers can contribute to financial education by incorporating it into employee benefits programs. Providing workshops, resources, and access to financial counseling can enhance employees' financial literacy and well-being.

Collaboration between governments, educational institutions, financial institutions, and nonprofit organizations is essential for a comprehensive and effective approach to financial education. Partnerships can leverage diverse expertise and resources to reach a broader audience.

Offering incentives for engaging in financial education can motivate individuals to actively participate in learning initiatives. Incentives could include discounts on financial products, tax benefits, or recognition for completing educational programs. Creating tangible benefits fosters a positive environment around financial education and encourages individuals to invest time and effort in enhancing their financial literacy.

Designing targeted financial education programs for vulnerable populations, such as low-income communities, immigrants, and underserved groups, is crucial. Tailoring educational content to address specific challenges and barriers faced by these populations ensures inclusivity and equity in access to financial knowledge.

Gamification involves incorporating game elements into educational content to make learning more engaging and interactive. Applying gamification principles to financial education can increase participation, boost motivation, and make complex financial concepts more accessible and enjoyable.

Governments play a pivotal role in advancing financial

education through policies and legislation. Implementing laws that mandate the inclusion of financial literacy in school curricula, promoting workplace financial education, and establishing standards for financial education programs contribute to a comprehensive and systemic approach.

Providing support for educators and financial counselors is essential for the effective delivery of financial education. Offering training programs, resources, and professional development opportunities ensures that those responsible for teaching financial literacy are well-equipped to engage and educate diverse audiences.

Integrating principles from behavioral economics into financial education programs acknowledges the psychological factors that influence financial decision-making. Understanding cognitive biases, decision heuristics, and emotional factors can enhance the effectiveness of financial education by addressing the behavioral aspects of financial choices.

Establishing metrics to measure the impact of financial education initiatives is crucial for ongoing improvement. Regular evaluations help identify successful strategies, areas for enhancement, and the overall effectiveness of financial education programs in achieving their intended outcomes.

Financial literacy is a global concern, and its status varies significantly across countries and regions. Some countries have made substantial progress in integrating financial education into their education systems and promoting awareness among citizens. However, challenges persist, particularly in developing regions where access to quality education and financial resources is limited.

Financial education and literacy serve as cornerstones for individual empowerment, economic stability, and societal progress. As individuals gain the knowledge and skills to make informed financial decisions, they contribute not only to their own well-being but also to the resilience and prosperity of communities and nations.

The challenges in promoting financial education are diverse and require multifaceted solutions, ranging from systemic changes in education systems to innovative approaches leveraging technology. Success stories from various countries demonstrate the positive impact of prioritizing financial literacy and integrating it into the fabric of society.

As we navigate an increasingly complex and interconnected global economy, the importance of financial education becomes even more pronounced. Governments, educational institutions, financial organizations, and communities must work collaboratively to foster a culture of financial literacy, ensuring that individuals are equipped to navigate the intricacies of personal finance and contribute to a more financially resilient and inclusive world.

Generational Money Perspectives

Generational money perspectives refer to the unique attitudes, beliefs, and behaviors toward money that are shaped by the experiences, events, and socio-economic conditions of a particular generation. Each generation, influenced by its historical context, societal changes, and economic circumstances, develops distinct financial values and approaches. In this exploration, we delve into the money perspectives of different generations, spanning from the Silent Generation to Generation Z, examining how their unique experiences have shaped their views on earning, spending, saving, and investing.

The Silent Generation, having lived through the Great Depression and World War II, developed a frugal and cautious approach to money. Shaped by economic hardships, scarcity, and the importance of saving for the future, many in this generation adopted conservative financial habits. Job stability and homeownership were highly prioritized, and debt was generally avoided. This generation's money perspective emphasizes financial security, stability, and a strong sense of duty to provide for their families.

The post-war Baby Boomers experienced economic growth, the rise of the middle class, and unprecedented prosperity. This generation witnessed the advent of credit cards and increased consumerism. Baby Boomers often pursued the "American Dream" of homeownership, higher education, and upward mobility. Many in this generation prioritize traditional financial goals like homeownership and retirement savings. However, they also faced challenges, such as economic recessions and market fluctuations, influencing their cautious optimism and desire for financial stability.

Generation X, often described as the "sandwich generation," faced unique challenges. They witnessed the rise of dual-income households, the advent of technology, and economic uncertainties. Many experienced the dot-com boom and bust, influencing their pragmatic and adaptable money perspective. Gen Xers tend to value independence, entrepreneurship, and are often skeptical of traditional financial institutions. This generation is known for being financially savvy, seeking a balance between saving for the future and enjoying the present.

Millennials came of age during the digital revolution, the Great Recession, and witnessed the transformative power of technology. This generation is characterized by a focus on experiences over possessions, a commitment to social and environmental issues, and a preference for flexibility in their careers. Millennials often carry significant student loan debt, influencing their cautious approach to credit and desire for financial transparency. They are more likely to embrace technology for managing finances, investing, and exploring alternative financial systems.

Generation Z, the first true digital natives, grew up in an era of smartphones, social media, and instant access to information. Early exposure to global challenges like climate change and economic inequality has shaped their values. Gen Zers are known for their entrepreneurial spirit, financial pragmatism, and a preference for experiences over material possessions. They are more likely to embrace alternative financial platforms, prioritize financial education, and seek socially responsible investment opportunities.

The economic conditions during a generation's formative years significantly impact their money perspectives. Periods of economic growth, recessions, or financial crises shape attitudes toward job security, debt, and risk tolerance.

The availability and adoption of technology influence how each generation interacts with money. For instance, the Silent Generation relied on traditional banking, while Millennials and Generation Z are more inclined toward digital banking, mobile payments, and cryptocurrencies.

Cultural changes, including shifts in societal norms, values, and expectations, play a role in shaping generational money perspectives. Evolving attitudes toward work, family structures, and individualism contribute to varying financial priorities.

Access to education and information has a profound impact on financial literacy and money management skills. Generations with greater access to educational opportunities may be more empowered to make informed financial decisions.

Major global events, such as wars, political movements, and pandemics, can shape a generation's outlook on money. These events often influence values, priorities, and approaches to financial planning.

Increasing awareness of social and environmental issues has influenced younger generations to prioritize ethical and sustainable financial practices. Millennials and Generation Z often seek investments aligned with their values and are more likely to support socially responsible businesses.

While each generation has its unique money perspective, there are common themes that transcend generational boundaries:

Across generations, there is a shared desire for financial security. Whether shaped by the hardships of the past or uncertainties of the future, individuals generally seek stability and a sense of control over their financial well-being.

The tension between enjoying the present and planning for the future is a universal theme. Each generation grapples with finding the right balance between spending on experiences today and saving for long-term goals like homeownership, education, and retirement.

The integration of technology into financial practices is a common thread. While older generations may adapt more slowly, there is a collective shift toward embracing digital tools for banking, investing, and financial management.

Economic uncertainties, whether driven by global events or market fluctuations, influence the financial behaviors of individuals across generations. Periods of economic downturns often result in increased financial caution and a focus on risk mitigation.

The importance of financial education is recognized across generations. As financial landscapes evolve, there is a shared acknowledgment of the need for ongoing learning to navigate complex financial systems and make informed decisions.

Open communication is crucial in navigating generational differences in money perspectives. Families and workplaces benefit from fostering an environment where individuals feel comfortable discussing their financial values, goals, and concerns.

Recognizing and adapting to evolving financial landscapes is essential. Institutions, businesses, and financial service providers need to adapt their offerings to meet the changing preferences and needs of different generations.

Promoting financial inclusion ensures that individuals from all generations have access to financial services, education, and opportunities. Addressing systemic barriers and tailoring services to diverse needs contribute to a more inclusive financial landscape.

In workplace settings, fostering collaboration among diverse generations can lead to a more inclusive and innovative financial culture. This may involve mentorship programs, cross-generational teams, and tailored financial wellness initiatives.

Financial institutions and service providers benefit from offering customized solutions that cater to the preferences and needs of different generations. This may involve flexible banking options, targeted investment products, and digital tools that align with diverse money perspectives.

As we look to the future, understanding generational money perspectives becomes increasingly important for various stakeholders – from policymakers and financial institutions to businesses and families. Several trends and considerations are likely to shape the financial landscapes of different generations:

Continued technological advancements will play a significant role in shaping the money perspectives of future generations. The integration of artificial intelligence, blockchain, and other emerging technologies may introduce new financial instruments and methods, influencing how individuals manage, invest, and transact with money.

Changes in work dynamics, driven by automation, remote work, and gig economies, will impact how individuals earn and manage their finances. The gig economy, in particular, may shape the financial habits of younger generations, emphasizing flexibility, entrepreneurship, and diversified income streams.

The growing emphasis on environmental and social responsibility is likely to continue influencing generational money perspectives. Future generations may place even greater importance on sustainable investing, ethical consumerism, and supporting businesses with a positive societal impact.

With increasing life expectancies, retirement planning will remain a crucial aspect of financial decision-making. Future generations may face the challenge of ensuring financial security throughout extended retirement periods, leading to innovative approaches to wealth management and retirement savings.

Unforeseen global events, such as economic recessions, pandemics, or geopolitical shifts, will continue to impact generational money perspectives. These events may prompt a reevaluation of financial priorities, risk management strategies, and approaches to building financial resilience.

Ongoing efforts to enhance financial education and literacy will be essential. Future generations will benefit from educational initiatives that equip them with the knowledge and skills needed to navigate evolving financial landscapes and make informed decisions.

Promoting inclusive financial practices will remain a priority. Bridging the gap between generations and ensuring that financial services cater to diverse needs will contribute to a more equitable and accessible financial system.

The increasing interconnectedness of individuals through digital platforms and the rise of digital identities will have implications for financial practices. Future generations may explore innovative ways to manage digital assets, embrace decentralized finance (DeFi), and navigate the complexities of digital transactions.

Lessons from past economic crises and global events underscore the importance of crisis preparedness. Future generations may adopt financial strategies that prioritize emergency funds, risk mitigation, and adaptability in the face of unexpected challenges.

Cultural and social shifts will continue to shape the values and priorities of future generations. Evolving attitudes toward work, family, and societal responsibilities may influence how individuals approach financial goals, philanthropy, and wealth distribution.

Generational money perspectives provide valuable insights into the diverse ways individuals approach finances based on the unique experiences and circumstances of their respective eras. While each generation exhibits distinct characteristics, common threads of financial security, balancing present enjoyment with future planning, and the importance of financial education run through the fabric of generational money perspectives.

As we move forward, it is crucial to recognize the dynamism inherent in these perspectives. The interplay of technological advancements, societal changes, economic conditions, and global events will continue to shape how individuals from different generations engage with money.

Stakeholders across various sectors – from educational institutions and financial service providers to employers and policymakers – play integral roles in fostering financial inclusivity, adapting to evolving needs, and promoting a deeper understanding of generational money perspectives. By acknowledging and addressing these perspectives, we contribute to a more nuanced and responsive financial landscape that empowers individuals of all ages to navigate their unique financial journeys.

Money and Well-Being

Money and well-being are intricately connected, with financial circumstances often playing a significant role in shaping individuals' overall life satisfaction and mental health. In this exploration, we delve into the complex relationship between money and well-being, examining how financial factors impact mental and emotional health, the role of income in subjective well-being, and the pursuit of a balanced and fulfilling life beyond monetary considerations.

Financial stress is a common source of anxiety for many individuals. Concerns about debt, job security, and the ability to meet financial obligations can contribute to heightened stress levels. Chronic financial stress may lead to anxiety disorders, affecting one's mental well-being and overall quality of life.

Economic hardship, such as job loss, foreclosure, or bankruptcy, is linked to an increased risk of depression. The psychological toll of financial struggles can manifest in feelings of hopelessness, helplessness, and a diminished sense of self-worth.

Financial difficulties can strain relationships, leading to conflicts and emotional distress. Couples often cite financial issues as a significant source of marital discord. The stress of managing finances, especially during challenging times, can create tension and affect the emotional well-being of individuals and their relationships.

The generational perspective on money and mental health varies. Older generations, shaped by experiences such as economic downturns and scarcity, may carry ingrained financial stressors. Younger generations, grappling with student loan debt and economic uncertainties, may face unique challenges in navigating their mental well-being amid financial pressures.

The relationship between income and subjective well-being is complex and subject to what is known as the Easterlin Paradox. This paradox suggests that while within a given society, individuals with higher incomes tend to report higher levels of well-being, the average level of well-being does not necessarily increase as a society becomes wealthier over time.

The concept of the hedonic treadmill suggests that individuals adapt to changes in their income levels, and the initial boost in well-being from increased income tends to be temporary. As individuals adjust to higher income, their expectations and desires often rise in tandem, maintaining a relatively stable level of subjective well-being.

Well-being is influenced by various factors beyond income. Social connections, meaningful relationships, a sense of purpose, and engagement in activities that bring joy contribute significantly to overall life satisfaction. Focusing solely on financial achievements may not necessarily lead to sustained well-being.

Relative income, or how one's income compares to others in society, plays a role in subjective well-being. Social comparison theory suggests that individuals tend to evaluate their well-being in comparison to others. Thus, perceptions of financial status relative to peers can impact overall life satisfaction.

The pursuit of a fulfilling life extends beyond material possessions. While financial stability is crucial for meeting basic needs, the relentless pursuit of material wealth without considering non-material aspects can lead to a sense of emptiness. Embracing experiences, personal growth, and relationships as essential elements of a meaningful life is a paradigm shift.

According to Self-Determination Theory, individuals have innate psychological needs for autonomy, competence, and relatedness. Focusing on these psychological needs, rather than purely material goals, contributes to a sense of well-being and fulfillment. Autonomy in decision-making, mastery in skills, and meaningful connections are vital for a balanced life.

Consumer culture, driven by the constant pursuit of acquiring more possessions, can have negative consequences on well-being. The pressure to conform to societal expectations regarding lifestyle and material success can lead to a cycle of overconsumption, debt, and dissatisfaction.

The minimalist movement advocates for simplifying one's life by decluttering both physical possessions and non-essential commitments. Embracing minimalism can contribute to increased well-being by shifting the focus from accumulating material goods to experiencing a more intentional and purposeful life.

Implementing effective budgeting and financial planning practices is foundational to financial well-being. Creating a budget helps individuals allocate resources, prioritize spending, and save for future goals. A clear financial plan provides a sense of control and reduces financial stress.

Building an emergency fund is crucial for financial resilience. Having a financial safety net allows individuals to navigate unexpected expenses without compromising their overall well-being. Financial resilience contributes to a sense of security and peace of mind.

Practicing mindful spending involves thoughtful consideration of purchases and aligning spending with values and priorities. Being intentional about consumption choices reduces the risk of impulsive and regrettable spending, promoting financial well-being.

Prioritizing experiences over material possessions has been linked to higher levels of well-being. Investing in travel, hobbies, and meaningful activities contributes to lasting memories and a sense of fulfillment beyond the temporary satisfaction derived from material acquisitions.

Financial education plays a pivotal role in improving well-being by empowering individuals with the knowledge and skills needed to make informed financial decisions. Understanding key financial concepts, such as budgeting, investing, and debt management, enhances financial literacy. As individuals become more confident in their financial capabilities, they are better equipped to navigate the complexities of personal finance and, subsequently, experience improved well-being.

Achieving a balance between work and personal life is essential for overall well-being. Career choices that align with one's values and passions contribute to job satisfaction and a sense of fulfillment. Prioritizing work-life balance helps prevent burnout and promotes mental and emotional well-being.

Building a supportive community and maintaining strong social connections are integral to well-being. In times of financial stress, having a network of friends, family, or community resources provides emotional support and practical assistance. Shared experiences and mutual support contribute to a sense of belonging and security.

Engaging in philanthropic activities and giving back to the community can enhance well-being. Research suggests that acts of kindness and generosity contribute to a positive sense of self and increased life satisfaction. Integrating philanthropy into financial practices fosters a broader perspective on wealth and its potential impact on others.

Practicing mindfulness in financial decision-making involves being fully present and aware of one's financial choices. Mindfulness helps individuals avoid impulsive decisions, manage emotions related to money, and make intentional choices aligned with their values. Mindful financial practices contribute to a healthier relationship with money.

Cultural values and perspectives play a significant role in shaping attitudes toward wealth and well-being. In some cultures, communal well-being may take precedence over individual financial success, emphasizing collective prosperity and interconnectedness.

Societal expectations and pressures related to success and material achievement can impact individuals' perceptions of well-being. Chasing external benchmarks of success may lead to a perpetual cycle of discontent, emphasizing the importance of aligning personal values with societal expectations.

Economic inequality within societies can contribute to disparities in well-being. Individuals facing economic hardships may experience lower levels of well-being compared to those with greater financial resources. Addressing systemic issues of inequality is crucial for promoting widespread well-being.

Government policies and societal initiatives can influence the well-being of citizens. Policies related to social safety nets, healthcare, education, and income support programs play a role in mitigating financial stress and promoting overall well-being. Advocacy for policies that prioritize holistic well-being is essential for societal progress.

The intricate relationship between money and well-being underscores the multidimensional nature of individuals' experiences with finances. While financial stability is undeniably important for meeting basic needs and achieving life goals, it is only one aspect of a broader picture of well-being.

Understanding the psychological and emotional impact of financial circumstances allows individuals to make intentional choices that prioritize their mental health and overall life satisfaction. Practices such as budgeting, mindful spending, and investing in experiences contribute to financial well-being, while considerations of work-life balance, social connections, and community engagement enrich overall well-being.

Cultural, societal, and systemic factors also play pivotal roles in shaping the intersection of money and well-being. Recognizing the influence of these external factors provides a context for understanding diverse perspectives and addressing broader issues related to economic inequality and societal expectations.

Ultimately, the pursuit of well-being extends beyond monetary considerations, emphasizing the importance of a balanced, purpose-driven life. By integrating financial practices that align with personal values, fostering supportive communities, and advocating for societal initiatives that prioritize well-being, individuals can navigate the complex interplay of money and well-being with greater resilience and fulfillment.

Financial Decision-Making
Under Stress

Financial decision-making under stress is a complex and challenging aspect of personal finance that profoundly influences individuals' lives. Whether facing unexpected financial emergencies, economic downturns, or personal crises, the ability to make sound financial decisions under stress is crucial for maintaining financial stability and well-being. In this exploration, we delve into the psychological aspects, common challenges, and strategies for effective financial decision-making when facing stressors.

Stress triggers physiological responses in the body, including the release of cortisol, a hormone associated with the body's "fight or flight" response. Elevated stress levels can impair cognitive function, affecting decision-making abilities. Individuals under stress may experience difficulties in concentration, memory, and logical reasoning, making it challenging to assess complex financial situations.

Stress often amplifies emotional responses, influencing financial decision-making. Fear, anxiety, and panic can lead to impulsive choices, such as selling investments hastily or making decisions based on short-term emotions rather than long-term goals. Understanding and managing emotional reactions are essential for making rational financial decisions under stress.

Cognitive biases, such as loss aversion and recency bias, become more pronounced under stress. Loss aversion, for example, refers to the tendency to fear losses more than the pleasure derived from equivalent gains. Recognizing and mitigating these biases is crucial for making objective financial decisions that align with one's overall financial strategy.

Persistent stress can lead to decision fatigue, wherein individuals become mentally exhausted from making numerous decisions. Decision fatigue can result in avoidance of financial decisions, procrastination, or making suboptimal choices. Simplifying financial decision-making processes and prioritizing critical choices can help alleviate decision fatigue.

Sudden emergencies, such as medical expenses, home repairs, or job loss, can create intense financial stress. The urgency of these situations may lead individuals to make hasty decisions without thoroughly evaluating their long-term consequences.

Economic downturns and market volatility can evoke stress for investors. The fear of financial losses may prompt individuals to make impulsive investment decisions, potentially undermining their long-term financial goals.

High levels of debt and financial strain contribute significantly to stress. Individuals dealing with overwhelming debt may struggle to prioritize and make decisions regarding debt repayment, leading to a cycle of increasing stress.

Major life transitions, such as divorce, retirement, or the death of a loved one, introduce significant financial considerations. Navigating these transitions under stress can be emotionally challenging, impacting one's ability to make well-informed financial decisions.

Limited financial resources require individuals to make trade-offs and prioritize their spending. Stress stemming from financial constraints may hinder the ability to allocate resources effectively and make decisions that align with long-term financial goals.

Building financial resilience involves creating a robust financial foundation that can withstand unexpected challenges. This includes establishing emergency funds, having adequate insurance coverage, and diversifying investments. A resilient financial plan provides a buffer during stressful situations.

Incorporating mindfulness and stress reduction techniques, such as meditation, deep breathing exercises, or yoga, can help manage stress levels. These practices enhance emotional regulation and improve cognitive function, supporting more thoughtful financial decision-making.

Consulting with financial professionals, such as financial advisors or counselors, can provide valuable insights and guidance during stressful periods. Professionals can offer objective perspectives, analyze financial options, and help individuals make informed decisions aligned with their long-term objectives.

Recognizing the impact of decision fatigue, individuals can prioritize essential financial decisions and tackle them systematically. Breaking down complex decisions into manageable steps reduces cognitive overload and facilitates more thoughtful choices.

Having clear financial goals serves as a guiding framework for decision-making. Clearly defined goals provide a sense of direction, helping individuals prioritize decisions that align with their overarching financial objectives.

Anticipating potential emergencies and having contingency plans in place can mitigate stress when unexpected events occur. Preparing for various scenarios, such as job loss or medical emergencies, enables individuals to make more rational decisions during challenging times.

Recognizing the tendency for impulsive actions under stress, individuals can implement mechanisms to slow down decision-making. This may involve imposing a waiting period before finalizing significant financial decisions to allow for thoughtful consideration.

Seeking support from friends, family, or support

networks can provide emotional assistance during stressful financial situations. Open communication allows individuals to share concerns, gain perspective, and receive advice from trusted sources.

A foundation of financial education empowers individuals to navigate financial challenges with greater confidence. Understanding basic financial concepts, such as budgeting, investing, and debt management, enhances decision-making skills under stress.

Consider an investor facing stress during a market downturn. Instead of succumbing to panic and selling investments, a long-term perspective guided by financial resilience and a diversified portfolio can lead to better outcomes. Historical market recoveries demonstrate the importance of patience and adherence to a well-thought-out investment strategy.

In the case of job loss, individuals who have established emergency funds and developed contingency plans are better equipped to navigate the financial implications. Having a financial safety net allows for a more thoughtful approach to managing expenses and seeking new employment opportunities.

Individuals grappling with high levels of debt may experience stress related to repayment decisions. Implementing debt repayment strategies, such as prioritizing high-interest debt and negotiating repayment terms, can alleviate financial strain and pave the way toward long-term financial health.

When facing major life transitions, such as retirement, individuals benefit from careful financial planning. Engaging with financial professionals to assess retirement income, healthcare needs, and estate planning can ease the stress associated with these transitions, ensuring a more secure financial future.

Financial decision-making under stress is a dynamic and multifaceted aspect of personal finance that requires a combination of psychological resilience, strategic planning, and informed decision-making. The interplay of cognitive, emotional, and situational factors underscores the complexity of navigating financial challenges during stressful periods.

By cultivating financial resilience, incorporating stress reduction techniques, seeking professional guidance, and prioritizing decision-making, individuals can enhance their ability to make sound financial choices under stress. Real-life examples demonstrate the positive impact of proactive financial strategies and the importance of a long-term perspective in preserving financial well-being.

Ultimately, recognizing the psychological and emotional aspects of financial decision-making under stress is crucial for developing effective coping mechanisms. Financial stress is an inherent part of life, and acknowledging its potential impact on decision-making allows individuals to proactively address challenges and build a more resilient financial mindset.

In conclusion, the intersection of stress and financial decision-making requires a holistic approach that considers both the emotional and cognitive dimensions. By integrating strategies to manage stress, seeking professional guidance when needed, and establishing a solid financial foundation, individuals can navigate turbulent financial waters with greater confidence and clarity. Financial well-being is not only about the numbers on a balance sheet but also about the peace of mind that comes from knowing one can make thoughtful decisions, even in the face of adversity.

The Role of Peer Pressure
and Social Comparison

The influence of social circles on financial behavior is a powerful and often underestimated factor shaping individuals' financial choices, habits, and attitudes. Human beings are inherently social creatures, and our interactions with friends, family, colleagues, and broader social networks play a significant role in shaping how we approach money. In this exploration, we delve into the various ways in which social circles influence financial behavior, examining the impact of social norms, peer pressure, financial conversations, and shared values on individual financial decisions.

Social norms are unwritten rules or expectations within a social group that influence individual behavior. In the context of finance, social norms dictate what is considered acceptable or expected behavior regarding spending, saving, and investing. Individuals often conform to these norms as a way to fit in and gain social approval.

Peer pressure can exert a powerful influence on financial behavior. In social circles where conspicuous consumption is prevalent, individuals may feel compelled to spend beyond their means to maintain a certain lifestyle. Conversely, in circles that prioritize frugality and savings, there may be pressure to conform to more conservative financial habits.

Social comparison, the act of evaluating oneself in relation to others, can contribute to lifestyle inflation. Seeing peers achieve certain financial milestones or adopt particular spending habits may create a desire to keep up or surpass, leading to increased spending and potential financial strain.

Individuals often derive a sense of identity from their social circles, and financial behavior becomes a part of this identity. For example, belonging to a group that values entrepreneurial endeavors may encourage risk-taking in financial ventures, while a group emphasizing stability may promote more conservative financial choices.

The level of openness regarding financial matters within a social circle can significantly impact individual financial behavior. In circles where financial conversations are encouraged, individuals may feel more comfortable seeking advice, sharing experiences, and learning from one another. This openness can contribute to informed decision-making.

Social circles can serve as informal platforms for financial education. Individuals may share insights, tips, and resources related to personal finance, contributing to the collective financial knowledge within the group. This shared education can influence financial behaviors positively.

The advice and opinions of peers often carry weight in financial decision-making. Individuals may turn to friends or colleagues for guidance on investment choices, major purchases, or financial planning. This peer advice can either reinforce existing financial behaviors or introduce new perspectives.

Financial behaviors can spread through social networks via a phenomenon known as behavioral contagion. If individuals observe their peers adopting specific financial habits, they may be more inclined to mimic those behaviors, leading to the replication of certain spending or saving patterns within the group.

Social circles are often formed around shared values, and financial values are no exception. Individuals tend to gravitate towards friends and associates who share similar attitudes toward money. This alignment of values can create a cohesive financial culture within the group.

Shared values extend to philanthropy and social impact within social circles. If a group places a high value on charitable giving or investing in socially responsible ventures, individuals are likely to align their financial choices with these shared priorities.

Social circles may develop collective financial goals or aspirations. Whether it's planning group vacations, joint investments, or shared business ventures, the alignment of financial objectives within a social group can influence individual decision-making to contribute to these shared goals.

Within social circles, individuals may form financial accountability partnerships. Friends or colleagues may set mutual financial goals, track each other's progress, and provide support and encouragement. These partnerships create a sense of shared responsibility for financial success.

Individuals often belong to multiple social circles, each with its own set of financial norms and influences. For example, a person may have a professional network, a family circle, and a group of friends. The diversity of these circles introduces a range of financial perspectives and behaviors.

Conflicts can arise when individuals navigate conflicting financial values within different social circles. For instance, a professional network emphasizing career advancement and high spending may clash with a family circle promoting financial stability and conservative choices.

Individuals often adapt their financial behaviors based on the social context. This adaptability can lead to variations in spending, saving, and investment patterns depending on the expectations and norms of a particular social circle.

Cultural backgrounds contribute significantly to the financial values within social circles. Individuals from diverse cultural backgrounds may bring unique perspectives on money management, wealth accumulation, and financial priorities, enriching the collective financial culture.

Negative peer influences, such as overspending or encouraging risky financial behaviors, pose challenges. Mitigation involves maintaining awareness of individual financial values, setting personal boundaries, and seeking support from like-minded individuals within the circle.

The pressure to conform to social norms can be addressed by fostering open communication about financial concerns and setting realistic expectations. Individuals can assert their financial boundaries while maintaining a healthy balance within the social group.

Educating individuals within social circles about financial literacy and empowerment is a proactive strategy. Shared knowledge can elevate the collective financial awareness of the group and empower individuals to make informed decisions aligned with their values.

Encouraging positive peer influences involves highlighting and celebrating responsible financial behaviors within the group. By promoting a culture of financial responsibility and success, individuals can inspire each other to make sound financial decisions.

The advent of social media has introduced a digital dimension to social influence on financial behavior. Individuals often share financial achievements, investment successes, and lifestyle choices on social platforms. The curated nature of these digital narratives can create a perception of financial success and prosperity, influencing others in the online social sphere.

Social media platforms facilitate constant comparison, potentially leading to a phenomenon known as "social media comparison syndrome." Individuals may feel pressure to showcase a certain lifestyle, including spending on luxury items or experiences, to keep up with their online peers. This can contribute to financial strain as people attempt to match the perceived success of their social media connections.

Social media also fosters digital financial communities where individuals can engage in conversations about money, share tips, and discuss financial goals. These online communities have both positive and negative influences, depending on the shared values and financial philosophies within the group.

While social media offers educational opportunities through financial influencers and experts, it also comes with risks. Misinformation, unrealistic portrayals of financial success, and the pressure to participate in certain spending trends can negatively impact financial decision-making.

Family is a primary social circle that significantly influences financial behavior. Inheritance patterns, financial philosophies passed down through generations, and family expectations can shape an individual's approach to money. Understanding and navigating these family dynamics is crucial for developing a healthy financial mindset.

Different generations may have distinct perspectives on debt, with older generations emphasizing financial conservatism and younger generations being more comfortable with leveraging credit. These generational differences within families can contribute to varied financial behaviors and attitudes toward debt.

Parents often play a pivotal role in shaping the financial values of their children. The transference of financial values, whether consciously or unconsciously, influences how individuals approach budgeting, saving, investing, and other financial decisions throughout their lives.

Balancing the expectations of different generations within a family can pose challenges. For instance, the desire to meet the financial expectations of older family members while aligning with the financial values of one's peer group can create internal conflicts and influence decision-making.

Actively promoting financial literacy within social circles is a constructive strategy. Organizing workshops, book clubs, or discussions on personal finance can enhance the financial knowledge of the group and foster positive financial behaviors.

Cultivating supportive networks that prioritize financial well-being provides individuals with encouragement and guidance. Surrounding oneself with like-minded individuals who share similar financial values can create a positive reinforcement loop.

Establishing collective financial goals within social circles encourages collaboration and accountability. Whether it's saving for a group vacation, starting a business together, or collectively investing, shared financial objectives strengthen the sense of unity and purpose within the group.

Fostering open communication about financial challenges, goals, and aspirations helps dispel myths and misconceptions within social circles. The more transparent and honest the conversations, the better equipped individuals are to make informed financial decisions.

Recognizing and embracing the diversity of financial perspectives within social circles is essential. Acknowledging that individuals may have different financial values, goals, and risk tolerances fosters a culture of acceptance and mutual respect.

As technology continues to shape the way people interact, the digital transformation will likely amplify the influence of social circles on financial behavior. Online communities, digital financial education platforms, and social media will play increasingly significant roles in shaping financial attitudes.

Globalization and increased cultural exchange may lead to the integration of diverse financial perspectives. Exposure to different cultural norms and financial practices through international connections can contribute to a more nuanced and adaptable approach to finance within social circles.

Economic trends and societal changes will impact the financial behaviors within social circles. For example, economic downturns may lead to shared financial challenges, prompting individuals to collaborate and support each other through difficult times.

Innovations in financial services, such as peer-to-peer lending, robo-advisors, and decentralized finance (DeFi), may introduce new ways for social circles to engage in financial activities collectively. These innovations could reshape traditional notions of financial collaboration and decision-making.

Educational institutions, employers, and governmental bodies will likely continue to play a crucial role in shaping financial education within social circles. Implementing comprehensive financial literacy programs can empower individuals to make informed decisions and positively influence their peers.

The influence of social circles on financial behavior is a multifaceted and dynamic aspect of personal finance. Whether through shared values, peer pressure, or digital interactions, individuals are constantly shaped by their social environments. Recognizing the impact of social influences allows individuals to navigate their financial journeys with greater awareness and intentionality.

As the landscape of social interactions continues to evolve with technological advancements and societal changes, fostering positive financial behaviors within social circles becomes increasingly important. By promoting financial literacy, building supportive networks, encouraging open communication, and embracing the diversity of perspectives, individuals can harness the positive aspects of social influence to enhance their financial well-being and contribute to the financial health of their communities.

The Power of Habits and Rituals in Money Management

The power of habits and rituals in money management is a profound and transformative force that significantly influences individuals' financial well-being. Habits and rituals shape our daily routines, providing a framework for decision-making, goal-setting, and overall financial behavior. In this exploration, we delve into the psychology behind habits, the impact of rituals on money management, and practical strategies for cultivating positive financial routines.

Habits operate within a loop of cue, routine, and reward. A cue triggers a habitual behavior, leading to a routine, which is followed by a reward. This loop becomes ingrained in our neural pathways, making habits automatic and often unconscious. Understanding this loop is essential for reshaping financial behaviors.

The brain's ability to adapt and reorganize itself, known as neuroplasticity, plays a crucial role in habit formation. As individuals consistently engage in a particular behavior, neural pathways strengthen, making the habit more automatic. This adaptability is both an opportunity and a challenge in shaping positive money habits.

Rewards reinforce habits by providing a sense of satisfaction or pleasure. In money management, positive rewards could include achieving financial goals, saving for future endeavors, or experiencing a sense of financial security. Identifying and incorporating rewarding elements is key to establishing lasting financial habits.

Habits extend beyond actions to influence thinking

patterns and decision-making. Individuals with positive financial habits tend to approach money-related decisions with a proactive and goal-oriented mindset. Conversely, negative habits may lead to impulsive decisions and financial stress.

Rituals are intentional, symbolic actions performed with a specific purpose. In money management, rituals can serve as powerful tools for creating a sense of order, discipline, and mindfulness. They go beyond habits by incorporating a deliberate and often ceremonial aspect into financial activities.

Rituals have a profound emotional impact, providing a sense of structure and meaning to financial actions. Whether it's a monthly budgeting ritual, a weekly financial review, or a daily gratitude practice for financial well-being, these rituals contribute to a positive emotional connection with money.

Rituals can be tailored to align with financial goals. For example, creating a ritual around debt repayment, such as a monthly celebration for reaching milestones, transforms the process into a positive and rewarding experience. Rituals enhance motivation and create a sense of accomplishment.

Financial rituals promote mindfulness by encouraging individuals to be present and intentional in their money-related activities. Whether it's setting financial intentions for the day, reflecting on spending choices, or expressing gratitude for financial stability, rituals cultivate awareness and consciousness.

Understanding the cues that trigger financial habits is the first step in reshaping them. Cues could be specific situations, emotional states, or even certain times of the day. By identifying these cues, individuals can intentionally modify their routines and responses to create positive financial habits.

Behavioral modification techniques, such as positive reinforcement and gradual changes, are effective in reshaping money habits. For instance, setting small, achievable financial goals and rewarding oneself for meeting them reinforces positive behavior and contributes to habit formation.

Keystone habits are foundational behaviors that have a positive ripple effect on other areas of life. Establishing a keystone habit in money management, such as regular budgeting or automated savings, can lead to improvements in overall financial well-being.

Regularly tracking financial progress and celebrating milestones are powerful motivators. Whether it's paying off a credit card, reaching a savings goal, or consistently sticking to a budget, acknowledging achievements reinforces positive financial habits and encourages continued effort.

Incorporating a daily financial reflection ritual involves taking a few moments each day to review spending, assess progress toward financial goals, and set intentions for the next day. This ritual fosters mindfulness and encourages proactive decision-making.

Designating a specific time each week for a budgeting ritual provides an opportunity to review income, expenses, and savings. This structured approach enhances financial organization and helps individuals stay on track with their financial plans.

Monthly financial check-ins serve as a ritual for a more comprehensive review of financial health. Individuals can assess their net worth, review investment portfolios, and adjust budgets as needed. This ritual promotes a strategic and forward-thinking approach to money management.

Rituals centered around setting financial intentions involve expressing positive affirmations or goals related to money. Whether done daily or weekly, this practice cultivates a positive mindset and reinforces a sense of purpose in financial actions.

Cultivating positive money habits and incorporating

rituals into financial routines can contribute to stress reduction and improved mental well-being. Knowing that there is a structured approach to managing finances and achieving financial goals provides a sense of control and reduces financial anxiety.

Positive money habits and rituals contribute to enhanced financial discipline. The consistent practice of budgeting, saving, and investing creates a disciplined approach to money management. This discipline translates into better financial decision-making and the ability to resist impulsive or unnecessary spending.

Achieving financial goals through the repetition of positive habits and rituals boosts financial confidence. As individuals witness the tangible results of their efforts, such as increased savings or debt reduction, they gain confidence in their ability to navigate and control their financial future.

The cumulative effect of positive money habits and rituals is long-term financial stability. Regular savings, disciplined spending, and intentional financial planning lay the foundation for a secure financial future. Individuals following these practices are better equipped to handle unexpected expenses and pursue long-term financial objectives.

Resistance to change is a common obstacle when trying to establish new financial habits. Overcoming this resistance involves starting with small, manageable changes and gradually expanding the scope of financial habits. Consistent effort and a focus on achievable goals help build momentum.

Lack of accountability can hinder the establishment of positive money habits. Seeking accountability from a trusted friend, family member, or financial advisor provides external support and encouragement. Sharing financial goals and progress with an accountability partner reinforces commitment.

Inconsistency in executing financial habits and rituals may arise from a busy schedule or competing priorities. Creating a realistic and flexible routine that aligns with one's lifestyle can help address this challenge. Consistency is more achievable when habits are integrated into existing daily or weekly routines.

Limited financial literacy may impede the development of effective money habits. Addressing this challenge involves investing time in financial education, seeking guidance from financial professionals, and leveraging online resources. A solid understanding of basic financial concepts empowers individuals to make informed decisions.

Cultural norms and values influence the formation of financial habits and rituals. In some cultures, communal financial practices and rituals, such as collective savings or financial ceremonies, play a significant role. Understanding and respecting cultural influences contribute to a more holistic approach to money management.

Societal expectations may shape the financial rituals individuals adopt. For instance, societal emphasis on consumerism may lead to spending-focused rituals, while a culture valuing frugality may promote savings-oriented rituals. Awareness of these influences allows individuals to make intentional choices aligned with their values.

Technological advancements influence the way individuals engage in financial habits and rituals. The convenience of mobile banking, budgeting apps, and automated savings tools has transformed the way people manage their money. Integrating technology into financial routines can enhance efficiency and accessibility.

Social media can both positively and negatively impact financial habits and rituals. On one hand, online communities can provide support and encouragement for positive financial practices. On the other hand, the constant exposure to others' financial achievements may lead to unhealthy comparisons and potentially detrimental financial behaviors.

Educational initiatives play a crucial role in promoting positive financial habits. Schools, workplaces, and community organizations can implement programs that teach fundamental financial concepts and encourage the development of healthy money habits from an early age.

Raising awareness about the benefits of incorporating rituals into money management fosters a cultural shift toward intentional financial practices. Campaigns, workshops, and online resources can highlight the emotional and psychological advantages of incorporating rituals into financial routines.

Ensuring accessibility to financial resources, including educational materials, budgeting tools, and advisory services, is essential. Financial institutions, governments, and non-profit organizations can collaborate to make these resources widely available, empowering individuals to enhance their financial habits.

Promoting financial inclusivity ensures that individuals from diverse backgrounds have access to resources that support the development of positive money habits. Tailoring financial education to address the specific needs of different communities contributes to a more inclusive and equitable approach to money management.

The future of financial habits and rituals is likely to be shaped by personalized financial technology solutions. AI-driven tools that analyze individual spending patterns, offer personalized budgeting advice, and automate savings based on financial goals will become increasingly prevalent.

Behavioral economics principles will continue to play a significant role in designing interventions that promote positive financial habits. Insights from behavioral science will be integrated into financial apps, educational programs, and workplace initiatives to effectively influence money-related behaviors.

The collaboration between financial institutions and technology companies will be pivotal in shaping the future landscape of financial habits and rituals. Partnerships may lead to the development of innovative tools, seamless integration of financial services, and personalized recommendations that cater to individual habits and preferences.

The evolving understanding of financial well-being will drive future initiatives. Beyond traditional financial success metrics, there will be an increased focus on holistic well-being, incorporating emotional, mental, and social aspects. Financial habits and rituals will be designed to enhance overall life satisfaction and fulfillment.

The power of habits and rituals in money management extends beyond the mere execution of financial tasks; it encompasses a transformative approach to one's relationship with money. By understanding the psychology of habits, integrating intentional rituals, and consistently practicing positive financial behaviors, individuals can shape a future of financial stability, confidence, and well-being.

As technology advances, societal attitudes evolve, and educational initiatives expand, the landscape of financial habits and rituals will continue to undergo transformation. The key lies in the conscious cultivation of habits that align with personal values, foster discipline, and contribute to long-term financial success. In this journey, individuals, institutions, and technology will play interconnected roles in reshaping the way we approach and manage money, ultimately leading to a more prosperous and fulfilling financial future.

Money and Personal Values

Money and personal values are intricately intertwined, forming a dynamic relationship that significantly influences individuals' lifestyles, choices, and overall well-being. The alignment between one's financial decisions and personal values is crucial for achieving a sense of fulfillment, purpose, and authenticity in life. In this exploration, we delve into the profound impact of personal values on money-related choices, the potential conflicts that may arise, and strategies for achieving harmony between financial decisions and deeply held values.

Personal values represent the core principles and beliefs that guide individuals in making decisions and shaping their behaviors. These values often serve as a moral compass, reflecting what is deemed important, meaningful, and fulfilling in life. Common personal values include integrity, honesty, family, freedom, and personal growth.

Personal values play a central role in decision-making across various aspects of life, including relationships, career choices, and, significantly, finances. The alignment of financial decisions with personal values ensures a congruent and purposeful approach to money management.

Personal values are subjective and vary among individuals. What holds great importance for one person may have lesser significance for another. This subjectivity contributes to the uniqueness of each person's value system and, consequently, their approach to handling money.

Personal values are not static; they can evolve over time based on experiences, growth, and changing perspectives. Life events, such as marriage, parenthood, or career shifts, may prompt a reevaluation of values and their role in shaping financial priorities.

The way individuals allocate their financial resources reflects their values. Whether it's prioritizing experiences over possessions, allocating funds for charitable giving, or investing in education, financial decisions become tangible expressions of one's deeply held beliefs.

Lifestyle choices, including housing, travel, and leisure activities, are often aligned with personal values. For example, someone valuing sustainability might invest in eco-friendly practices, while a person prioritizing family may allocate resources for shared experiences and quality time together.

Career choices and financial aspirations are closely connected to personal values. Individuals driven by a sense of purpose may prioritize job satisfaction over high salaries, while those valuing financial security may pursue stable and lucrative career paths.

Consumer behavior is a manifestation of personal values. The products and services individuals choose to buy, the companies they support, and the causes they endorse through their purchasing decisions all reflect their values and contribute to shaping their identity.

External influences, such as societal expectations, advertising, and peer pressure, can introduce conflicting messages that challenge personal values. The pressure to conform to certain lifestyles or spending patterns may create tension between societal norms and individual values.

Mismatched financial goals within relationships or families can lead to conflicts. For instance, if one partner values adventure and spontaneity while the other prioritizes financial security, finding common ground and reconciling these differing values becomes crucial for financial harmony.

Unconscious spending, driven by impulse or societal pressures, can result in misalignment with personal values. Individuals may find themselves investing in possessions or experiences that, upon reflection, do not contribute to their authentic sense of fulfillment.

Pursuing a career solely for financial gain without considering personal fulfillment can lead to dissatisfaction. The conflict arises when financial success is prioritized at the expense of aligning one's career with intrinsic values and a sense of purpose.

Engaging in reflective self-assessment is the foundational step in aligning money and values. Individuals should identify and articulate their core values, considering what brings them fulfillment, purpose, and a sense of meaning in both the short and long term.

Prioritizing values in financial planning involves consciously incorporating personal beliefs into budgeting, saving, and investment decisions. This may include allocating funds for experiences that align with values, contributing to causes that matter, or making ethical investment choices.

Open communication is essential in relationships to ensure shared understanding and alignment of financial values. Regular discussions about financial goals, priorities, and individual values contribute to mutual respect and the ability to navigate potential conflicts.

Adopting mindful spending practices entails making intentional and conscious choices about expenditures. Before making purchases, individuals can reflect on whether the expense aligns with their values and contributes to their overall well-being.

In situations where conflicts arise, seeking compromises and finding common ground is essential. This may involve finding creative solutions that allow for the pursuit of individual values within the constraints of shared financial goals.

Seeking financial counseling or guidance can provide individuals and couples with tools to navigate conflicts and align financial decisions with values. Professional advice can offer insights into budgeting, financial planning, and strategies for finding harmony between money and values.

Values and financial priorities evolve, and it's crucial to recognize the need for continuous reevaluation and adaptation. Regularly assessing whether financial choices align with current values allows for adjustments and ensures ongoing harmony between money and personal beliefs.

Mindfulness practices, such as meditation and reflection, can contribute to greater awareness of the link between money and values. These practices enhance emotional intelligence and decision-making, fostering a deeper connection with personal values in financial choices.

When money and values are aligned, individuals experience a heightened sense of purpose and fulfillment. Financial decisions that resonate with personal values contribute to a more meaningful and purpose-driven life.

Alignment between money and values reduces financial stress. Knowing that financial decisions are in harmony with one's authentic beliefs creates a sense of control and minimizes the anxiety associated with conflicting priorities.

In relationships, shared values and aligned financial goals enhance satisfaction and strengthen the connection between partners. The ability to navigate conflicts and compromise based on shared values fosters a sense of unity and mutual support.

The positive impact of aligned money and values extends to mental and emotional well-being. Individuals experience less internal conflict, greater self-awareness, and a more positive relationship with money when their financial choices reflect their deepest values.

Cultural influences play a significant role in shaping attitudes toward money and values. Cultural norms may dictate the importance placed on certain financial goals, such as homeownership, family support, or educational pursuits. Understanding and navigating these cultural expectations is crucial in aligning personal values with broader societal influences.

Societal values, often influenced by consumer culture, can impact individual attitudes toward money. The emphasis on materialism and external markers of success may create tension for individuals who value more intrinsic qualities, such as relationships, personal growth, or community engagement. Resisting societal pressures and staying true to one's values requires a mindful and intentional approach.

Economic factors, including income inequality and economic instability, can influence personal values. Individuals facing financial challenges may prioritize security and stability, while those in more affluent circumstances may have the luxury to focus on values related to philanthropy or personal fulfillment. Recognizing the impact of economic factors on values allows for a more nuanced understanding of financial choices.

In an interconnected world, global perspectives on wealth and values come into play. Different cultures may have varying attitudes toward accumulation, spending, and philanthropy. As individuals navigate a globalized landscape, considering diverse perspectives contributes to a more comprehensive understanding of the relationship between money and values.

Financial education initiatives can play a pivotal role in promoting values-based finance. Integrating discussions about personal values, ethical considerations, and the societal impact of financial choices into educational programs equips individuals with the tools to align their money decisions with their values.

Ethical investing aligns financial choices with values by directing investments toward companies and industries that share similar ethical principles. Educational efforts promoting awareness about ethical investing empower individuals to consider the social and environmental impact of their financial portfolios.

Corporate social responsibility (CSR) initiatives influence the alignment of money and values. Individuals may choose to support companies that demonstrate a commitment to social and environmental causes aligned with their values. Companies, in turn, recognize the growing importance of aligning their practices with societal values.

The rise of sustainable and values-driven business models reflects a broader shift toward conscious consumerism. Businesses that prioritize environmental sustainability, social responsibility, and ethical practices resonate with individuals seeking to align their purchasing power with their values.

Technology is likely to play an increasingly significant role in values-based finance. Fintech innovations, such as apps that track spending based on ethical considerations or platforms facilitating impact investing, will empower individuals to make financial choices in line with their values.

Blockchain technology has the potential to enhance transparency in financial systems. Transparent financial systems can provide individuals with clearer insights into the ethical practices of financial institutions, supporting values-based decision-making.

Social movements advocating for environmental sustainability, social justice, and ethical business practices will continue to influence values-based finance. As these movements gain momentum, individuals may become more conscious of the societal impact of their financial decisions.

Policy and regulatory frameworks will shape the future landscape of money and values. Governments and regulatory bodies may implement measures to encourage ethical financial practices, disclosure of environmental and social impacts, and responsible corporate behavior. These considerations can further support individuals in aligning their financial choices with their values.

A growing emphasis on financial well-being, beyond traditional measures of success, will influence the future relationship between money and values. Individuals, institutions, and policymakers may prioritize holistic approaches that consider the emotional, mental, and societal impact of financial decisions.

The intricate interplay between money and personal values is a dynamic force that shapes the way individuals navigate their financial journeys. Recognizing the influence of personal values on financial choices empowers individuals to make decisions that resonate with their authentic selves, fostering a sense of purpose and fulfillment.

As societal norms, cultural expectations, and technological advancements continue to evolve, the future of money and values holds exciting possibilities. The integration of values into financial education, the rise of ethical investing, and the growing impact of social movements underscore a shifting landscape where individuals increasingly seek to align their financial choices with their deeply held beliefs.

Ultimately, the journey towards harmonizing money and values is a personal and ongoing process. By reflecting on personal values, engaging in open communication, and staying attuned to the broader societal context, individuals can navigate the complexities of the modern financial world with a sense of authenticity, purpose, and fulfillment.

The Fear of Financial Failure

The fear of financial failure is a pervasive and powerful emotion that can profoundly impact individuals' lives, influencing their decisions, behaviors, and overall well-being. This fear often stems from concerns about one's ability to meet financial obligations, achieve financial goals, and secure a stable future. In this exploration, we delve into the psychological aspects of the fear of financial failure, its origins, its impact on individuals and society, and strategies for overcoming and managing this fear.

The fear of financial failure has deep psychological roots, often intertwining with basic human needs for security, stability, and a sense of control. This fear can manifest in various ways, such as anxiety about debt, worry about job security, or fear of not being able to provide for oneself and loved ones. Understanding these psychological underpinnings is essential in addressing the fear effectively.

Socioeconomic factors, including upbringing, cultural influences, and societal expectations, contribute to the development of the fear of financial failure. Individuals from backgrounds where financial struggles were prevalent may carry a heightened fear of repeating those patterns. Societal pressures to achieve certain financial milestones can also intensify this fear.

The rise of social media and constant connectivity has led to increased comparison among individuals. Seeing others' perceived financial successes can exacerbate the fear of financial failure, fostering a sense of inadequacy and pressure to conform to societal standards. Social influence plays a significant role in shaping financial fears and aspirations.

The uncertainty of the future, coupled with economic instability, contributes to the fear of financial failure. Global economic fluctuations, job market volatility, and unexpected life events create an atmosphere of unpredictability, amplifying concerns about financial security and success.

The fear of financial failure takes a toll on mental and emotional health. Persistent worry about money can lead to stress, anxiety, and, in severe cases, depression. The constant preoccupation with financial concerns may interfere with overall well-being, affecting sleep, relationships, and overall life satisfaction.

Individuals driven by the fear of financial failure may exhibit risk-averse behavior in decision-making. The reluctance to take calculated risks, whether in investments, career choices, or entrepreneurial pursuits, can hinder personal and financial growth. Fear-driven decision-making often results in missed opportunities.

Financial fears can strain relationships, especially when partners have differing attitudes toward money. Communication breakdowns, arguments over financial priorities, and feelings of inadequacy can contribute to tension within relationships. The fear of being a financial burden on others may lead individuals to isolate themselves emotionally.

The chronic stress associated with the fear of financial failure can have physical health consequences. Increased levels of stress hormones may contribute to conditions such as high blood pressure, cardiovascular problems, and compromised immune function. The intricate connection between financial stress and physical health underscores the holistic impact of this fear.

Some individuals cope with the fear of financial failure through escapism and avoidance. This may involve ignoring financial issues, procrastinating on important decisions, or engaging in behaviors such as overspending or compulsive shopping as a temporary distraction from financial concerns.

The fear of financial failure can drive individuals to overwork in an attempt to secure financial stability. While this dedication may yield short-term benefits, it often leads to burnout, negatively impacting mental and physical health. Overworking as a response to financial fears is a common pattern in today's competitive and fast-paced world.

Denial and financial ignorance are coping mechanisms rooted in avoiding the reality of financial challenges. Some individuals may choose to remain uninformed about their financial situation, accumulating debt or neglecting savings, in an effort to temporarily suppress the fear. However, this approach only exacerbates long-term financial issues.

Seeking quick fixes, such as participating in risky investments or gambling, is another response to the fear of financial failure. Individuals driven by the urgency to alleviate financial concerns may engage in high-risk activities, hoping for immediate financial relief. This behavior often leads to further financial instability.

One of the foundational steps in overcoming the fear of financial failure is increasing financial literacy. Understanding basic financial concepts, budgeting, and investment strategies empowers individuals to make informed decisions and gain a sense of control over their financial lives.

Seeking professional guidance from financial advisors or counselors can provide individuals with personalized strategies for overcoming financial fears. These professionals can assess individual circumstances, offer tailored advice, and create realistic financial plans that address fears and goals.

Mindfulness practices and stress management techniques are effective tools in addressing the emotional impact of financial fears. Techniques such as meditation, deep breathing exercises, and mindfulness-based stress reduction can help individuals cultivate a calm and centered approach to financial challenges.

Gradual exposure to financial challenges, combined with goal setting, allows individuals to confront their fears in manageable steps. Breaking down larger financial goals into smaller, achievable tasks builds confidence and diminishes the overwhelming nature of financial concerns.

Changing perspectives on success and failure is a transformative step in overcoming the fear of financial failure. Rather than viewing setbacks as permanent failures, individuals can reframe them as learning opportunities and stepping stones toward financial growth and resilience.

Defining personal success metrics that go beyond traditional financial markers is crucial. Focusing on aspects such as personal growth, relationships, and overall well-being provides a more holistic view of success, reducing the pressure associated with narrow financial definitions.

Cultivating a growth mindset involves embracing challenges and viewing failures as opportunities for learning and improvement. Individuals with a growth mindset are more resilient in the face of setbacks and are better equipped to navigate the uncertainties of financial journeys.

The ability to embrace flexibility and adaptability is key in overcoming the fear of financial failure. Life is inherently unpredictable, and financial plans may need adjustments along the way. Embracing change and adapting to evolving circumstances fosters a proactive and empowered approach to financial challenges.

Open communication with loved ones is crucial in overcoming the fear of financial failure. Sharing fears, concerns, and financial goals with trusted individuals fosters a supportive environment. Loved ones can provide encouragement, understanding, and collaborative problem-solving.

Community and peer support play a significant role in overcoming the fear of financial failure. Joining communities or support groups where individuals share similar financial concerns can provide a sense of belonging and understanding. Peer support offers the opportunity to exchange advice, strategies, and encouragement, creating a network of individuals navigating similar challenges.

Building a professional network and seeking mentorship can contribute to overcoming financial fears in a career context. Engaging with mentors who have successfully navigated similar challenges provides valuable insights, guidance, and a sense of reassurance. Learning from others' experiences can instill confidence in facing financial uncertainties.

Employee Assistance Programs (EAPs) often offer resources and support for employees dealing with various life stressors, including financial concerns. Accessing these programs can provide counseling services, financial education, and assistance in navigating challenging financial situations.

Applying mindfulness to budgeting and spending involves cultivating awareness of financial choices. Individuals can practice mindful spending by consciously considering their purchases, aligning them with priorities and values. This approach reduces impulsive decisions and contributes to a more intentional relationship with money.

Cultivating gratitude practices can shift the focus from financial fears to appreciation for current resources and opportunities. Regularly expressing gratitude for financial stability, supportive relationships, and personal accomplishments fosters a positive mindset and reduces the anxiety associated with the fear of financial failure.

Visualization and goal setting are powerful tools in overcoming financial fears. Creating a vivid mental image of desired financial outcomes and setting achievable goals provides motivation and direction. Visualization techniques help individuals envision success, creating a positive and proactive mindset.

Regular financial check-ins involve consistently reviewing and assessing one's financial situation. This practice allows individuals to stay informed, identify areas that require attention, and make adjustments as needed. Proactive engagement with financial matters contributes to a sense of control and confidence.

Building emergency funds is a fundamental aspect of financial resilience. Having a financial safety net provides a sense of security and a buffer against unexpected expenses. Accumulating savings for emergencies alleviates the fear of being unprepared for unforeseen financial challenges.

Diversifying income streams contributes to financial resilience by reducing dependence on a single source of income. Exploring additional avenues, such as side hustles, freelance work, or investments, provides individuals with a more robust financial foundation and a sense of empowerment.

Insurance and risk management strategies play a role in mitigating financial fears related to unexpected events. Adequate insurance coverage, including health, property, and life insurance, provides a level of financial protection. Understanding and managing risks contribute to a more secure financial outlook.

Continuous learning about personal finance, investments, and economic trends contributes to financial preparedness. Staying informed allows individuals to adapt to changing circumstances, make informed decisions, and navigate financial challenges with confidence.

Empowering individuals through financial education is a transformative step in overcoming the fear of financial failure. Educational initiatives that teach practical money management skills, budgeting, and investment strategies empower individuals to take control of their financial destinies.

Promoting financial inclusion ensures that individuals from diverse backgrounds have access to resources and opportunities. Overcoming financial fears requires addressing systemic barriers and providing equitable access to financial education, services, and opportunities for all.

Encouraging entrepreneurship and innovation fosters a spirit of self-reliance and creativity. Empowering individuals to explore entrepreneurial ventures, pursue innovative solutions, and take calculated risks contributes to a culture of financial resilience and growth.

Advocating for mental health support in the context of financial fears is essential. Acknowledging the psychological impact of financial concerns and promoting access to mental health resources helps individuals address the emotional aspects of financial challenges.

The fear of financial failure is a complex emotion with profound implications for individuals' lives. Overcoming this fear requires a multifaceted approach that encompasses financial education, psychological well-being, support systems, and proactive strategies for resilience. By understanding the roots of financial fears, adopting mindfulness practices, building a supportive network, and empowering individuals through education and preparation, it is possible to transform the fear of financial failure into a catalyst for growth, resilience, and financial well-being.

Financial Empowerment
and Independence

Financial empowerment and independence are integral components of personal well-being, providing individuals with the autonomy to make informed financial decisions, pursue their goals, and navigate the complexities of the economic landscape. In this exploration, we delve into the essence of financial empowerment and independence, examining the psychological, social, and economic dimensions that contribute to these empowering states. We will explore the key principles, challenges, and strategies that individuals can employ to achieve and sustain financial empowerment and independence.

Financial empowerment is a state where individuals have the knowledge, skills, and confidence to take control of their financial lives. It goes beyond income levels and material wealth, encompassing the ability to make informed decisions, set and achieve financial goals, and adapt to changing circumstances. Financial empowerment is a journey that involves continuous learning, self-awareness, and a proactive approach to financial well-being.

Financial Literacy: A strong foundation in financial literacy equips individuals with the knowledge to understand financial concepts, manage money effectively, and make informed choices.

Financial Planning: The ability to create and implement a financial plan is crucial for achieving long-term goals. Financial planning involves budgeting, saving, investing, and strategically managing resources.

Goal Setting: Financial empowerment is closely tied to goal setting. Individuals identify short-term and long-term financial goals, creating a roadmap for their financial journey.

Risk Management: Understanding and managing financial risks, such as emergencies, unexpected expenses, and market fluctuations, is a key aspect of financial empowerment.

Income Diversification: Financially empowered individuals often explore multiple income streams, reducing dependence on a single source of income and enhancing financial resilience.

At the core of financial empowerment is a sense of self-efficacy—the belief in one's ability to achieve financial goals. Building confidence through financial education, successful money management, and overcoming challenges contributes to a positive psychological foundation for financial empowerment.

Financial empowerment grants individuals autonomy over their financial decisions. It involves the ability to assess options, make choices aligned with personal values and goals, and take responsibility for the outcomes. Autonomy in decision-making is a key psychological aspect of feeling in control of one's financial destiny.

Financial empowerment addresses and alleviates financial anxiety. Through education, planning, and a proactive approach, individuals can reduce the stress associated with financial uncertainties and gain a sense of security.

Financial empowerment often involves a mindset shift from scarcity to abundance. Rather than focusing on limitations, individuals cultivate a mindset of abundance that emphasizes opportunities, possibilities, and a positive outlook on financial growth.

Gender dynamics play a significant role in financial empowerment. Historically, women have faced disparities in financial access and opportunities. Empowering women financially involves addressing these disparities, promoting financial education, and creating an inclusive environment for economic participation.

Cultural norms and values shape individuals' attitudes toward money and financial decisions. Financial empowerment initiatives must consider cultural diversity and tailor strategies to resonate with different cultural perspectives on money, saving, and wealth accumulation.

Social networks and community support contribute to financial empowerment. Individuals benefit from sharing experiences, gaining insights, and receiving support from their communities. Community-based financial education programs and resources enhance social capital and contribute to collective financial empowerment.

Achieving widespread financial empowerment requires addressing systemic inequities. Efforts to reduce income inequality, improve access to education, and create economic opportunities for marginalized communities contribute to a more inclusive and equitable financial landscape.

A cornerstone of financial empowerment is investing in financial education. Individuals, regardless of their background or income level, benefit from understanding basic financial concepts, budgeting, saving, investing, and managing debt. Financial education provides the knowledge needed to make informed decisions.

Setting clear and achievable financial goals is a fundamental strategy for empowerment. Goals provide direction, motivation, and a framework for decision-making. Whether saving for an emergency fund, homeownership, education, or retirement, defining goals helps individuals prioritize their financial efforts.

Budgeting is a practical tool for managing money effectively. Creating a budget involves categorizing income and expenses, allocating funds to various needs and goals, and tracking spending. Regularly reviewing and adjusting the budget ensures alignment with financial objectives.

An emergency fund serves as a financial safety net, providing a cushion for unexpected expenses or disruptions in income. Building and maintaining an emergency fund is a proactive strategy that enhances financial resilience and reduces the impact of unforeseen challenges.

Financial empowerment often involves diversifying income streams. This may include exploring side hustles, investments, or entrepreneurial ventures. Diversification reduces dependence on a single income source and enhances financial stability.

Long-term investing is a strategy for wealth accumulation and financial security. Individuals can invest in diversified portfolios, retirement accounts, and other financial instruments aligned with their risk tolerance and long-term goals. Compound growth over time contributes to financial independence.

Real estate and property ownership are avenues for building wealth. Whether through homeownership or real estate investments, property ownership can provide long-term financial stability and asset growth.

Entrepreneurship and small business ownership empower individuals to create income opportunities on their terms. Starting a business, freelancing, or pursuing entrepreneurial ventures allows individuals to leverage their skills and passions for financial success.

Effectively managing and reducing debt is a common challenge on the path to financial empowerment. Strategies include prioritizing high-interest debt, negotiating favorable repayment terms, and adopting disciplined repayment plans.

Financial illiteracy is a barrier to empowerment. Addressing this challenge involves promoting financial education at various levels, from schools to community programs. Governments, businesses, and nonprofits can contribute to initiatives that enhance financial literacy.

Economic uncertainties, such as job loss or market fluctuations, can pose challenges to financial empowerment. Building a robust emergency fund, diversifying income, and developing adaptable financial plans are strategies to navigate these uncertainties.

Systemic barriers, including discrimination and inequitable access to resources, can impede financial empowerment. Advocacy efforts are crucial for dismantling these barriers. Collaborative initiatives that address systemic inequalities, promote inclusive economic policies, and create opportunities for marginalized communities contribute to a more equitable path to financial empowerment.

Technology plays a pivotal role in advancing financial empowerment, particularly in the context of digital financial inclusion. Accessible banking services, mobile payment platforms, and online financial education resources broaden financial access and empower individuals to participate in the digital economy.

Fintech solutions provide tools for efficient financial management. Budgeting apps, investment platforms, and digital financial advisors offer user-friendly interfaces that simplify complex financial tasks, making financial empowerment more accessible to a broader audience.

Blockchain technology has the potential to enhance financial inclusion and transparency. Decentralized finance (DeFi) platforms built on blockchain enable individuals to access financial services without traditional intermediaries, fostering greater financial autonomy and independence.

Ensuring cybersecurity and consumer protection is essential for maintaining trust in digital financial tools. Robust cybersecurity measures and regulations safeguard individuals' financial information, fostering a secure environment for technology-driven financial empowerment.

Financial independence is the state where individuals have accumulated enough wealth and passive income to cover their living expenses without relying on active employment income. It represents a higher level of financial autonomy, allowing individuals to pursue their preferred lifestyle and goals.

Achieving financial independence involves a combination of saving, investing, and strategic decision-making. Individuals pursuing financial independence often follow principles such as the FIRE movement (Financial Independence, Retire Early), emphasizing frugality, high savings rates, and early investments for accelerated wealth accumulation.

Passive income streams are a key element of financial independence. These may include dividends from investments, rental income from real estate, royalties from intellectual property, or other sources that generate income with minimal ongoing effort. Diversifying passive income streams enhances financial resilience.

Financial independence often aligns with early retirement aspirations. Individuals pursuing financial independence have the flexibility to retire early and design their lifestyles based on personal preferences. This may involve travel, pursuing hobbies, or engaging in meaningful activities without the constraints of traditional employment.

Financial independence is subject to market fluctuations and investment risks. Economic downturns can impact investment portfolios, affecting the sustainability of passive income streams. Individuals pursuing financial independence must consider risk management strategies and maintain a diversified investment approach.

Healthcare costs and long-term expenses are critical considerations in the journey to financial independence. Adequate planning for healthcare needs, insurance coverage, and potential long-term care expenses ensures that individuals maintain financial security throughout their lives.

Achieving financial independence requires balancing present enjoyment with future security. Individuals must make decisions about spending, saving, and lifestyle that align with their values and long-term goals, considering both immediate satisfaction and future financial well-being.

Financial independence is not a static state; it involves evolving goals and adaptability. Individuals may reassess their financial plans based on changing circumstances, goals, or market conditions. Flexibility and the ability to adapt to new financial realities are crucial for sustained financial independence.

Financially empowered individuals contribute to community-level empowerment. Sharing knowledge, resources, and mentorship within communities amplifies the impact of financial empowerment initiatives. Grassroots efforts to enhance financial literacy and access to economic opportunities foster a culture of empowerment.

Financially empowered individuals often engage in philanthropy and social responsibility. Having the means to contribute to charitable causes, support community initiatives, or invest in socially responsible projects aligns with the broader impact of financial empowerment on societal well-being.

Financially empowered individuals may choose to pursue entrepreneurship, leading to job creation and economic growth. Entrepreneurial endeavors contribute to local economies, create employment opportunities, and stimulate innovation, fostering a positive cycle of financial empowerment within communities.

Individuals who experience financial empowerment

often become advocates for economic inclusion. Recognizing the transformative impact of financial autonomy, they may actively support policies and initiatives that promote economic equity, financial education, and opportunities for all.

Financial empowerment and independence represent more than just economic well-being; they encompass a holistic approach to personal and societal flourishing. As individuals gain the knowledge, skills, and confidence to navigate the financial landscape, they not only enhance their own lives but also contribute to the broader fabric of economic empowerment within communities.

Through education, strategic planning, technological advancements, and a commitment to addressing systemic inequities, financial empowerment becomes a catalyst for positive social change. The journey towards financial independence, with its emphasis on passive income, adaptability, and balancing present enjoyment with future security, reflects a paradigm shift in how individuals envision and pursue financial well-being.

As societies embrace the principles of financial empowerment and independence, the ripple effects extend beyond individual success to collective prosperity, fostering a more equitable and inclusive economic landscape for current and future generations.

The Role of Technology in
Money Management

In the fast-evolving landscape of personal finance, technology has become a powerful ally for individuals seeking to manage their money effectively, make informed decisions, and achieve financial wellness. This intersection of finance and technology has given rise to innovative tools, applications, and platforms that simplify, automate, and enhance various aspects of money management. In this exploration, we delve into the multifaceted role of technology in money management, examining its impact on budgeting, saving, investing, financial education, and the broader landscape of personal finance.

The evolution of money management technology represents a shift from traditional, manual methods to digital solutions. Historically, individuals relied on paper-based budgets, ledgers, and physical banks. The digital era has brought forth a wave of advancements that leverage computing power, connectivity, and data analytics to revolutionize how people interact with their finances.

The advent of online banking marked a significant milestone in money management. It allowed individuals to check account balances, transfer funds, and pay bills from the comfort of their homes. Digital transactions, facilitated by electronic payment systems and mobile apps, streamlined financial activities and eliminated the need for physical currency in many transactions.

Fintech (financial technology) companies emerged as disruptors in the financial industry, introducing innovative solutions that leverage software and technology to provide financial services. These companies addressed gaps in traditional banking, offering alternatives in areas such as lending, payments, investment management, and personal finance.

The rise of mobile wallets and contactless payments transformed how people make purchases. With the integration of smartphones into daily life, individuals could store payment information digitally, enabling swift and secure transactions through near-field communication (NFC) technology. This shift toward digital wallets contributed to the acceleration of a cashless society.

Personal finance apps have become indispensable tools for budgeting and expense tracking. These apps, often accessible on smartphones and other devices, empower users to create budgets, categorize expenses, and gain insights into their spending patterns. Examples include Mint, YNAB (You Need A Budget), and PocketGuard.

Automation features within budgeting apps streamline financial tasks. Users can set up automatic categorization of transactions, recurring bill payments, and savings transfers. Notifications and alerts keep users informed about their financial activities, upcoming bills, and deviations from budgeted targets, fostering proactive money management.

Money management apps leverage data visualization and analytics to present financial information in an easily digestible format. Graphs, charts, and reports help users visualize their financial health, track progress toward goals, and identify areas for improvement. This visual representation enhances financial literacy and decision-making.

Seamless integration with bank accounts and credit cards is a hallmark of effective budgeting apps. By syncing financial accounts, these apps provide real-time updates on balances and transactions. This integration eliminates the manual entry of data, saving time and reducing the likelihood of errors in financial tracking.

Robo-advisors are automated investment platforms that use algorithms to create and manage diversified investment portfolios. These platforms, such as Wealthfront and Betterment, offer cost-effective and user-friendly investment solutions. Robo-advisors leverage technology to assess risk tolerance, rebalance portfolios, and optimize investment strategies.

Micro-investing apps cater to individuals who want to invest small amounts of money. These apps enable users to invest spare change from everyday transactions by rounding up purchases to the nearest dollar. Acorns and Stash are examples of micro-investing apps that leverage technology to make investing accessible to a broader audience.

The advent of blockchain technology gave rise to cryptocurrency platforms that allow individuals to buy, sell, and trade digital assets. Cryptocurrency exchanges and wallets leverage secure blockchain networks, providing users with new avenues for investment. The decentralized nature of cryptocurrencies adds a layer of transparency and security.

Technology has facilitated the integration of financial planning and goal-based investing. Platforms like Personal Capital use sophisticated algorithms to analyze financial situations, project future scenarios, and align investment strategies with individual goals. This integration enhances the personalized and goal-oriented nature of modern money management.

Technology has democratized access to financial education through online courses and webinars. Platforms like Coursera, Khan Academy, and Udemy offer courses on various financial topics, empowering individuals to enhance their financial literacy from the comfort of their homes.

Personalized learning platforms use adaptive technology to tailor educational content to individual learning styles and preferences. This approach is particularly effective in financial education, where personalized learning journeys can cover topics ranging from basic budgeting to advanced investment strategies.

Financial literacy begins early, and technology has introduced educational apps designed to teach children about money. These apps use gamification and interactive experiences to instill foundational financial concepts, such as saving, spending, and the value of money.

Financial simulations and virtual reality (VR) experiences offer immersive learning opportunities. Individuals can engage in virtual scenarios that simulate real-world financial decisions, honing their skills in a risk-free environment. VR applications provide a unique dimension to financial education by creating lifelike scenarios.

Biometric authentication, such as fingerprint recognition and facial recognition, enhances the security of financial transactions. Mobile banking apps and digital wallets leverage biometrics to verify users' identities, adding an extra layer of protection against unauthorized access.

Two-factor authentication adds an additional security step beyond traditional passwords. Users receive a one-time code through a secondary channel, such as a text message or authentication app, to confirm their identity. 2FA reduces the risk of unauthorized access, especially in online banking and financial applications.

Encryption technologies ensure secure communication between users and financial platforms. End-to-end encryption protects sensitive information, including personal and financial data, from interception or unauthorized access. Secure communication protocols contribute to building trust in online financial transactions.

Machine learning algorithms play a crucial role in fraud detection. Financial institutions and platforms leverage these algorithms to analyze patterns, detect anomalies, and identify potentially fraudulent activities. Real-time monitoring powered by machine learning enhances the ability to prevent and respond to fraud.

AI-powered financial assistants, such as chatbots and virtual assistants, provide users with personalized financial insights. These assistants leverage artificial intelligence to analyze users' financial data, answer queries, and offer tailored recommendations. They may provide insights into spending patterns, suggest budget adjustments, and offer tips for achieving specific financial goals.

Predictive analytics use historical data and machine learning to anticipate future financial behaviors. This technology can forecast spending trends, identify potential savings opportunities, and provide users with proactive insights into their financial future. By understanding patterns and trends, individuals can make more informed decisions.

Behavioral finance insights utilize psychological principles to analyze and understand users' financial behaviors. By integrating behavioral finance concepts, technology can provide personalized recommendations that align with an individual's financial attitudes, risk tolerance, and decision-making patterns.

Personal Financial Management (PFM) tools aggregate financial data from various accounts to offer a comprehensive view of an individual's financial landscape. These tools, such as Intuit's Mint, empower users to track income, expenses, and net worth in one centralized platform. PFM tools contribute to a holistic understanding of one's financial standing.

The future of money management may see increased adoption of blockchain technology and decentralized finance (DeFi) platforms. Blockchain, with its secure and transparent nature, can revolutionize transaction processes, and DeFi platforms may offer decentralized lending, borrowing, and investment opportunities.

Artificial intelligence will likely play an even more significant role in predictive modeling. Advanced AI algorithms may provide individuals with highly accurate predictions of their financial future, helping them make more strategic decisions and plan for long-term goals with greater precision.

Voice-activated financial services powered by natural language processing are emerging as a convenient and accessible way to interact with money management tools. Users can inquire about their financial status, initiate transactions, or receive financial advice using voice commands, enhancing the accessibility of financial services.

The future may witness the development of personalized financial ecosystems, where various financial services seamlessly integrate to offer a unified and tailored experience. This could involve the integration of banking, investment, insurance, and budgeting tools within a single platform, providing users with a cohesive and personalized financial environment.

The increased reliance on technology in money management raises concerns about data security and privacy. Financial institutions and technology providers must prioritize robust cybersecurity measures to safeguard users' sensitive information and build trust in digital financial services.

Ensuring digital inclusion is a critical consideration as technology advances in money management. Efforts should be made to bridge the digital divide and make digital financial services accessible to individuals of all socioeconomic backgrounds, including those with limited access to technology.

The use of algorithms in financial services introduces the risk of bias, as algorithms may perpetuate or amplify existing societal biases. It is crucial to address algorithmic bias and ensure fairness in the design and deployment of technology to prevent discriminatory outcomes.

As technology becomes more integral to money management, addressing educational gaps and promoting technological literacy is essential. Individuals need the knowledge and skills to navigate digital financial tools effectively and make informed decisions in the rapidly evolving technological landscape.

The role of technology in money management has evolved from basic online banking to sophisticated AI-powered financial assistants and blockchain-based financial ecosystems. The ongoing integration of technology in personal finance brings numerous benefits, including enhanced convenience, improved decision-making, and increased accessibility to financial services.

While embracing these technological advancements, it is crucial to address challenges related to data security, digital inclusion, algorithmic bias, and educational gaps. Striking a balance between innovation and responsible implementation is key to ensuring that technology continues to empower individuals in their money management journey while minimizing potential risks.

As we look to the future, the continued development of cutting-edge technologies, such as blockchain, AI, and voice-activated services, holds the promise of further transforming how individuals manage their money. Ultimately, the synergy between finance and technology will shape a more connected, accessible, and personalized financial landscape for individuals across the globe.

Financial Resilience and Preparedness

In an ever-changing economic landscape marked by uncertainties, the concept of financial resilience and preparedness has gained prominence. Financial resilience is the ability of individuals and households to withstand and recover from economic shocks, while financial preparedness involves proactive measures taken to mitigate risks and build a robust financial foundation. This exploration delves into the key components of financial resilience, strategies for financial preparedness, and the importance of cultivating these qualities in the face of economic challenges.

Financial resilience refers to the capacity to endure financial setbacks, adapt to changing circumstances, and recover from economic challenges. It involves a combination of financial practices, behavioral traits, and adaptive strategies that enable individuals and households to navigate economic downturns with greater ease. The key components of financial resilience include emergency savings, diversified income sources, debt management, and a mindset focused on long-term financial well-being.

A fundamental aspect of financial resilience is the presence of emergency savings. This financial cushion serves as a buffer during unexpected events such as job loss, medical emergencies, or unforeseen expenses. Individuals with robust emergency funds are better positioned to weather financial storms without resorting to high-interest debt or depleting long-term savings.

Relying on a single income source can leave individuals

vulnerable to economic shocks. Financial resilience involves diversifying income streams, which could include additional part-time work, freelance opportunities, or passive income from investments. Diversification not only enhances financial stability but also provides a safety net in case of job loss or industry-specific downturns.

Effectively managing debt is a critical component of financial resilience. Individuals with manageable levels of debt and a strategic approach to repayment are better positioned to handle economic uncertainties. This involves understanding and prioritizing debts, negotiating favorable terms when possible, and avoiding high-interest debt that can erode financial stability.

Financial resilience is closely tied to one's mindset and behavioral traits. Individuals with a proactive and adaptable mindset tend to fare better in the face of financial challenges. Resilient individuals are more likely to view setbacks as temporary, seek solutions, and embrace a long-term perspective in their financial decision-making.

A cornerstone of financial preparedness is building and maintaining an emergency fund. Financial experts often recommend having three to six months' worth of living expenses set aside in a readily accessible account. Regular contributions to this fund, even in small amounts, can accumulate over time and provide a financial safety net.

Financial preparedness starts with a clear understanding of income, expenses, and financial goals. Creating a budget helps individuals allocate their resources effectively, identify areas for potential savings, and track spending patterns. Regularly reviewing and adjusting the budget ensures alignment with changing circumstances and priorities.

Insurance plays a crucial role in financial preparedness. Adequate coverage, including health insurance, property insurance, and life insurance, safeguards against unexpected events that could otherwise lead to significant financial strain. Evaluating and updating insurance policies as needed ensures that individuals are adequately protected.

Actively seeking opportunities to diversify income sources enhances financial preparedness. This could involve exploring side hustles, freelance work, or investments that generate passive income. Diversification not only increases overall income but also reduces reliance on a single source, making individuals more resilient to income disruptions.

Continuous learning and skill development contribute to financial preparedness by enhancing employability and adaptability. Acquiring new skills or staying current in one's field increases the likelihood of securing employment or finding alternative income opportunities during economic downturns.

Addressing and reducing debt is a proactive step in financial preparedness. Strategies may include prioritizing high-interest debts, consolidating loans for better terms, negotiating with creditors, and avoiding the accumulation of unnecessary debt. A strategic approach to debt management builds a stronger financial foundation.

Investing is a key element of financial preparedness that involves growing wealth over the long term. Individuals can allocate a portion of their savings to investments such as stocks, bonds, or retirement accounts. While investments carry risks, a diversified and well-managed portfolio can contribute to long-term financial resilience.

Economic uncertainties are inherent in the modern globalized world. Financial resilience and preparedness empower individuals to navigate these uncertainties with greater confidence and stability. Whether facing job loss, market downturns, or unexpected expenses, individuals with strong financial foundations are better equipped to weather the storm.

Financial stress is a significant contributor to overall

stress and anxiety levels. Having a robust financial plan and emergency fund alleviates the anxiety associated with financial uncertainties. Individuals with a sense of financial security are more likely to experience better mental well-being and focus on other aspects of their lives.

Financial resilience and preparedness are essential for safeguarding long-term financial goals. Whether saving for education, homeownership, or retirement, a well-prepared financial foundation ensures that individuals can stay on track even when faced with unexpected challenges. This protection of long-term goals contributes to a more secure financial future.

One of the risks of lacking financial preparedness is the potential reliance on high-interest debt to cover unexpected expenses. Accumulating credit card debt or resorting to payday loans can lead to a cycle of financial hardship. Prepared individuals can avoid these pitfalls by tapping into emergency savings instead.

Life is dynamic, and individuals may face circumstances that require lifestyle changes, such as relocating for a job opportunity or adapting to new family dynamics. Financial resilience provides the flexibility to navigate such changes without causing severe financial strain. It allows individuals to embrace opportunities and make decisions aligned with their values and aspirations.

Governments and institutions play a role in promoting financial resilience through education programs. Financial literacy initiatives provide individuals with the knowledge and skills needed to make informed financial decisions, manage risks, and plan for the future. These programs aim to empower individuals to take control of their financial well-being.

Robust social safety nets, including unemployment benefits, welfare programs, and affordable healthcare, contribute to financial resilience at the societal level. These support systems provide a safety net for individuals facing economic hardships, reducing the overall impact of economic downturns on vulnerable populations.

Governments implement regulations and consumer protections to ensure fair and transparent financial practices. These measures help prevent predatory lending, fraudulent schemes, and other practices that can undermine financial stability. Regulatory frameworks contribute to a more secure financial environment for individuals and households.

Ensuring access to financial services is crucial for promoting financial resilience. Governments and institutions work towards improving financial inclusion, providing individuals with access to banking services, affordable credit, and other financial tools. This inclusivity facilitates individuals' ability to save, invest, and protect themselves against financial shocks.

Cultural attitudes toward saving and financial planning can influence individual financial resilience. Societies that emphasize saving for the future and maintaining financial preparedness contribute to a collective mindset of stability and resilience. Cultural practices that encourage responsible financial behaviors play a role in shaping individuals' approaches to money management.

Community support systems, including family networks and community organizations, can provide an additional layer of financial resilience. In some cultures, there is a strong emphasis on mutual support during times of need. These support systems can act as a safety net, offering assistance and resources to individuals facing financial challenges.

Societal attitudes toward financial challenges and setbacks can impact individuals' mental health. Reducing the stigma associated with financial difficulties encourages open discussions about financial well-being. This cultural shift fosters a supportive environment where individuals feel more comfortable seeking help and taking proactive steps to improve their financial resilience.

Formal education plays a crucial role in building financial resilience. Integrating financial education into school curricula equips individuals with foundational knowledge about budgeting, saving, investing, and managing debt. Early exposure to financial concepts fosters a lifelong understanding of responsible money management.

Financial education should extend beyond formal schooling into adulthood. Providing opportunities for continuing education on financial topics ensures that individuals stay informed about evolving financial landscapes, investment options, and strategies for adapting to economic changes. Adult education programs, workshops, and online resources contribute to ongoing financial literacy.

To promote financial resilience for all, educational resources must be accessible and inclusive. Governments, educational institutions, and financial organizations can collaborate to create resources that cater to diverse audiences, considering varying levels of financial literacy, cultural backgrounds, and socioeconomic status. This inclusivity ensures that everyone has access to essential financial knowledge.

In the digital age, digital financial literacy is increasingly important. Individuals need to understand online banking, digital payment methods, and the potential risks associated with digital financial transactions. Educational programs should address digital literacy to empower individuals to navigate the digital financial landscape securely.

Singapore has been recognized for its comprehensive approach to financial education. The government, along with financial institutions, has implemented various programs targeting different age groups. These programs cover topics such as budgeting, saving, investing, and retirement planning. The aim is to equip individuals with the knowledge and skills needed to make informed financial decisions.

India has seen the success of microfinance initiatives that empower individuals in low-income communities to build financial resilience. Microfinance institutions provide small loans, financial education, and support for income-generating activities. This approach has proven effective in promoting entrepreneurship and reducing vulnerability to economic shocks.

Kenya's success in mobile banking and financial inclusion has contributed to enhanced financial resilience. Mobile money platforms, such as M-Pesa, have expanded access to financial services, allowing individuals in remote areas to save, transfer money, and access credit. These initiatives empower communities by providing them with essential financial tools.

One of the challenges in promoting financial resilience is overcoming barriers to access. Some individuals, particularly those in marginalized communities, may face obstacles such as limited access to banking services, lack of financial infrastructure, or inadequate educational resources. Efforts should focus on addressing these barriers to ensure widespread financial inclusion.

The rapid pace of technological advancements presents both opportunities and challenges. While digital tools can enhance financial education and access, there is a need to ensure that individuals can navigate these technologies safely and securely. Ongoing efforts are required to adapt educational programs to incorporate digital financial literacy.

In an interconnected global economy, events in one part of the world can have ripple effects globally. Economic shocks, such as recessions or financial crises, can impact individuals regardless of their geographical location. Efforts to promote financial resilience should consider the implications of global economic integration and provide individuals with tools to navigate these complexities.

Climate change poses significant financial risks, including extreme weather events, resource scarcity, and shifts in market dynamics. Individuals and communities need to be prepared for the financial implications of climate-related challenges. Financial education programs should incorporate awareness of climate-related risks and strategies for adapting to a changing environment.

Financial resilience and preparedness are fundamental pillars of individual and societal well-being, especially in the face of economic uncertainties. Building and sustaining financial resilience involves a combination of education, proactive planning, and adaptive strategies. Governments, institutions, and communities play pivotal roles in creating an environment that supports financial resilience through accessible education, social safety nets, and inclusive financial services.

As societies continue to evolve in an increasingly interconnected and dynamic world, the importance of cultivating financial resilience becomes even more pronounced. By prioritizing financial education, reducing barriers to access, and fostering a culture of proactive financial management, individuals and communities can navigate economic uncertainties with greater confidence and build a foundation for long-term financial well-being.

The Influence of Advertising and Marketing

I n the contemporary landscape, advertising and marketing wield significant influence, shaping consumer behavior, perceptions, and choices. These pervasive forces are omnipresent, infiltrating our daily lives through various channels, from traditional media to the digital realm. This exploration delves into the intricate dynamics of advertising and marketing, examining their impact on consumer psychology, societal trends, ethical considerations, and the evolving landscape in the age of digital media.

Advertising operates at the intersection of psychology and commerce, leveraging insights into consumer behavior to influence purchasing decisions. Psychologists and marketing experts collaborate to decode the factors that drive consumer choices, exploring concepts such as motivation, perception, and learning to create compelling campaigns that resonate with target audiences.

Emotions play a pivotal role in consumer decision-making. Successful advertising often relies on emotional appeals, aiming to evoke feelings that forge a connection between the consumer and the brand. Whether through humor, nostalgia, or empathy, advertisers strategically craft messages to elicit emotional responses that can shape brand perception and loyalty.

Perception, or how individuals interpret and make sense of information, is a cornerstone of advertising effectiveness. Marketers employ design, visuals, and storytelling techniques to influence how products are perceived. By framing products in a certain light, advertisers seek to create positive associations that influence consumers' perceptions and preferences.

Branding is a powerful tool that goes beyond individual advertisements. It involves creating a distinct brand identity that encapsulates values, personality, and positioning in the market. Consistent branding fosters recognition, trust, and loyalty among consumers. Successful brands become synonymous with specific qualities, influencing consumer choices even in a crowded market.

The landscape of advertising has undergone a profound transformation with the rise of digital media. While traditional channels such as television, radio, and print advertising still hold sway, digital platforms, including social media, online streaming, and influencer marketing, have emerged as dominant forces. The shift to digital enables advertisers to target specific demographics with unprecedented precision and tailor messages for maximum impact.

Social media influencers have become central figures in contemporary advertising. These individuals, often with large and engaged followings, collaborate with brands to promote products authentically. Influencer marketing capitalizes on the trust and rapport influencers build with their audiences, creating a more personalized form of advertising that aligns with the dynamics of social media relationships.

Native advertising seamlessly integrates with the content surrounding it, blurring the lines between editorial and promotional material. This approach seeks to provide value to the audience while subtly promoting a product or service. Native advertising is prevalent on digital platforms, including sponsored content on news websites or integrated promotions in social media feeds.

The era of big data has ushered in an era of personalized and targeted advertising. Advertisers leverage data analytics and algorithms to tailor advertisements based on users' preferences, behaviors, and demographics. This precision targeting aims to deliver messages that resonate with individual consumers, increasing the likelihood of engagement and conversion.

Advertising plays a pivotal role in shaping cultural norms and values. Advertisements often reflect and reinforce societal ideals, influencing perceptions of beauty, success, and social acceptance. Conversely, advertising can also challenge norms and contribute to cultural shifts by promoting diversity, inclusivity, and social responsibility.

Critics argue that advertising contributes to a culture of consumerism and materialism. The constant barrage of messages urging consumers to acquire more can cultivate a mindset of perpetual desire and dissatisfaction. Advertisements can create aspirations linked to material possessions, influencing individuals to associate personal fulfillment with the acquisition of products.

In contrast, advertising can be a force for positive change by aligning with social causes. Brands increasingly engage in purpose-driven marketing, using their platforms to advocate for social and environmental issues. Advertisements that champion sustainability, equality, and social justice contribute to a broader cultural conversation and may influence consumers to support brands aligned with their values.

Ethical considerations in advertising extend beyond the content of campaigns to issues of transparency, truthfulness, and responsible messaging. Deceptive advertising practices, false claims, and manipulative techniques raise ethical concerns. Regulators and industry bodies play a role in establishing guidelines and standards to ensure that advertising aligns with ethical principles.

Cognitive biases influence how individuals process information, and advertisers leverage these biases to their advantage. Anchoring, for example, involves presenting an initial piece of information (such as a high price) that influences subsequent judgments. In advertising, anchoring can impact consumers' perceptions of product value and pricing.

The scarcity principle suggests that people place a higher value on items that are perceived as scarce or in limited supply. Advertisers often use scarcity and urgency tactics to create a sense of FOMO (fear of missing out), encouraging consumers to act quickly. Limited-time offers and "while supplies last" promotions capitalize on this cognitive bias.

Social proof, a cognitive bias where individuals look to others for guidance on how to behave, is a driving force in influencer marketing. The popularity and endorsement of products by influencers serve as social proof, influencing followers to adopt similar preferences and behaviors. The psychological impact of social proof extends to product reviews, testimonials, and user-generated content.

Confirmation bias, the tendency to favor information that confirms existing beliefs or preferences, is harnessed by advertisers to reinforce brand loyalty. Once consumers have positive associations with a brand, they are more likely to seek out information that supports their positive perceptions and ignore or downplay information that contradicts their views.

The integration of augmented reality (AR) and virtual reality (VR) presents new avenues for immersive advertising experiences. AR and VR technologies allow brands to create interactive and engaging campaigns, offering consumers a more personalized and hands-on interaction with products and services.

The rise of voice search and smart assistants has implications for advertising strategies. Brands need to optimize their content for voice search and explore opportunities to engage with consumers through voice-activated devices. The conversational nature of voice interactions requires a shift in advertising tactics to align with this emerging trend.

Growing concerns about data privacy have prompted increased scrutiny of advertising practices. Consumers are becoming more conscious of how their data is collected, used, and shared. Establishing transparent data practices and prioritizing consumer trust will be crucial for advertisers to maintain positive relationships with their audience.

Interactive content and gamification are becoming prominent trends in advertising. Brands are incorporating interactive elements into their campaigns, such as quizzes, polls, and games, to enhance user engagement. This approach not only captures attention but also encourages active participation, creating a more memorable and enjoyable advertising experience.

Ephemeral content, characterized by its temporary nature, has gained popularity on platforms like Snapchat and Instagram Stories. Advertisers are leveraging this format to create short-lived, engaging narratives. Storytelling remains a powerful tool in advertising, allowing brands to connect emotionally with their audience and communicate a cohesive brand narrative.

Artificial intelligence (AI) and predictive analytics are revolutionizing advertising by enabling more accurate targeting and personalized recommendations. AI algorithms analyze vast amounts of data to predict consumer behavior and preferences, allowing advertisers to deliver tailored content and recommendations. This data-driven approach enhances the effectiveness of advertising campaigns.

As advertising becomes more pervasive, consumers have responded by adopting ad-blocking tools and expressing resistance to intrusive advertising. Ad-blocking software allows users to filter out unwanted ads, signaling a shift in consumer behavior towards more control over their online experience. Advertisers must navigate this landscape by creating non-intrusive, relevant, and engaging content.

The rise of ad-free platforms and subscription-based models is altering the traditional advertising landscape. Streaming services, news websites, and other platforms are increasingly adopting subscription models to provide ad-free experiences in exchange for a fee. This trend challenges advertisers to find innovative ways to reach audiences on platforms that prioritize user subscriptions.

User-generated content (UGC) has become a powerful force in advertising, emphasizing authenticity and genuine connections. Brands encourage consumers to create and share content related to their products, fostering a sense of community and trust. Authenticity in advertising is increasingly valued by consumers, who seek genuine experiences over traditional, polished marketing messages.

Influencer marketing, while still impactful, is evolving to address issues of trust and authenticity. Consumers are becoming discerning about sponsored content, and influencers are under scrutiny to maintain credibility. As a result, advertisers are moving towards long-term partnerships with influencers, focusing on authentic collaborations that align with both the influencer's brand and the values of their audience.

With the advent of digital advertising, brands can reach global audiences more easily. However, achieving resonance in diverse cultural contexts requires a nuanced approach. Successful global advertising involves not only translating content but also understanding and respecting cultural nuances. Brands must prioritize localization to ensure their messages are relevant and culturally sensitive.

Consumers increasingly demand cultural diversity and inclusivity in advertising. Brands are recognizing the importance of representing diverse perspectives in their campaigns, reflecting the multicultural reality of their audience. Inclusive advertising not only fosters positive brand perception but also resonates with consumers who seek representation and authenticity.

Global advertising requires a careful consideration of cultural taboos and sensitivities. What may be acceptable in one culture could be offensive in another. Advertisers must conduct thorough research and collaborate with local experts to navigate cultural nuances, avoiding unintentional missteps that could harm brand reputation.

Advertising and marketing wield unparalleled influence in shaping consumer behavior, cultural norms, and societal trends. The interplay of psychology, technology, and cultural dynamics continues to evolve, presenting both opportunities and challenges for advertisers. The future of advertising lies in the ability to adapt to emerging trends, respect consumer preferences, and embrace ethical practices that prioritize transparency and authenticity.

As we navigate the complex landscape of advertising, it becomes imperative for brands to not only capture attention but also build lasting connections with consumers. The balance between data-driven personalization and respect for privacy, the evolution of storytelling in a digital era, and the recognition of diverse cultural perspectives are key considerations. Ultimately, the effectiveness of advertising will be defined by its ability to resonate with consumers in meaningful ways while acknowledging the evolving expectations of an empowered and discerning audience.rs must navigate the delicate balance between personalized

Generosity and Giving

Generosity, the act of giving without expecting something in return, is a profoundly human quality that transcends cultural, social, and economic boundaries. While generosity undoubtedly benefits recipients, its impact extends far beyond the act of giving. This exploration delves into the psychological benefits of generosity, uncovering how acts of kindness, altruism, and charitable behavior contribute to the well-being of individuals and communities.

Engaging in generous acts triggers the release of neurotransmitters in the brain associated with pleasure and reward. The phenomenon known as the "helper's high" describes the euphoric feeling experienced by individuals after performing a generous act. Neurotransmitters like dopamine and endorphins contribute to an increased sense of well-being and happiness.

Oxytocin, often referred to as the "love hormone" or "bonding hormone," plays a crucial role in social connections. Acts of generosity, particularly those involving interpersonal relationships, stimulate the release of oxytocin. This fosters a sense of connection, trust, and bonding between individuals, enhancing the quality of relationships and promoting overall emotional well-being.

Generosity has been linked to a reduction in stress levels. Engaging in altruistic acts can lower cortisol, the stress hormone, contributing to a calmer and more relaxed state of mind. The physiological benefits of reduced stress extend to improved cardiovascular health and immune function, highlighting the holistic impact of generosity on overall well-being.

Numerous studies have shown a positive correlation between altruistic behavior and mental well-being. Individuals who regularly engage in acts of generosity report higher levels of life satisfaction, happiness, and a sense of purpose. Altruism provides a meaningful avenue for individuals to contribute to the greater good, fostering a positive mindset and a sense of fulfillment.

Generosity has been identified as a potential antidote to depression and anxiety. The focus on others and the act of giving can shift attention away from personal challenges, providing individuals with a sense of purpose beyond their own concerns. This redirection of focus, coupled with the positive emotions associated with generosity, contributes to mental health resilience.

In times of personal adversity, engaging in acts of generosity can serve as a coping mechanism. Giving to others, whether through time, resources, or support, provides individuals with a proactive and constructive outlet for managing stress and adversity. This coping strategy fosters a sense of agency and resilience in the face of life's challenges.

Generosity cultivates empathy, the ability to understand and share the feelings of others. By actively participating in acts of kindness and generosity, individuals develop a heightened awareness of the needs and experiences of those around them. This increased empathy strengthens social bonds and contributes to a more compassionate and interconnected society.

Acts of generosity have a ripple effect, influencing not only the immediate recipients but also observers and those indirectly impacted. Witnessing acts of kindness can inspire individuals to emulate similar behavior, creating a positive feedback loop of generosity. This ripple effect contributes to the overall social and emotional fabric of communities.

Generosity within interpersonal relationships serves as

a powerful model for healthy and supportive dynamics. Whether in friendships, family, or romantic partnerships, acts of generosity foster an environment of mutual care and consideration. Partners who engage in generous behaviors towards each other contribute to the longevity and satisfaction of their relationships.

Generosity provides individuals with a sense of purpose beyond personal achievement or material pursuits. Contributing to the well-being of others, whether through charitable donations, volunteer work, or simple acts of kindness, instills a profound sense of meaning and significance. This connection to a larger purpose contributes to a more fulfilled and purpose-driven life.

Engaging in acts of generosity can positively impact self-esteem. The recognition of one's ability to make a difference, no matter how small, fosters a positive self-image and a sense of efficacy. Generosity reinforces the idea that individuals have the capacity to contribute positively to the lives of others, reinforcing their intrinsic value and worth.

Generosity is a dynamic force that evolves across the lifespan. In youth, acts of kindness contribute to the development of empathy and social skills. In adulthood, generosity becomes intertwined with career choices, parenting, and community engagement. In later life, individuals often find purpose and fulfillment in acts of generosity, leaving a legacy that extends beyond their lifetime.

Generosity is a cornerstone of community building. When individuals within a community actively engage in generous acts, whether through volunteering, charitable giving, or supporting local initiatives, the collective well-being of the community is enhanced. Generosity fosters a sense of shared responsibility and solidarity, strengthening the fabric of communities.

Volunteering, a tangible expression of generosity, has

been associated with increased social integration. Individuals who volunteer regularly often experience a sense of belonging, expanded social networks, and a greater connection to their communities. Volunteerism contributes not only to the well-being of recipients but also to the social cohesion of the volunteers themselves.

Generosity extends to the workplace, influencing organizational culture and employee well-being. Companies that prioritize philanthropy, employee volunteering programs, and a culture of generosity often experience increased employee satisfaction, engagement, and loyalty. Generosity in the workplace fosters a positive environment where individuals feel valued and connected to a shared mission.

Educational environments play a crucial role in shaping individuals' values and behaviors. Incorporating lessons and activities that emphasize generosity, empathy, and kindness can contribute to the development of socially responsible and compassionate individuals. Educational institutions are increasingly recognizing the importance of nurturing these qualities alongside academic achievements.

Service-learning programs, which combine academic learning with community service, offer students the opportunity to actively engage in acts of generosity. Beyond academic benefits, service-learning contributes to character development, instilling values such as empathy, responsibility, and a commitment to social justice.

Viewing generosity as a life skill underscores its importance in the holistic development of individuals. Teaching generosity as a skill involves imparting the knowledge, attitudes, and behaviors associated with giving. By embedding generosity into educational curricula, educators contribute to the cultivation of future generations capable of making positive contributions to society.

While generosity offers numerous psychological benefits,

individuals must strike a balance between giving to others and prioritizing self-care. Overextending oneself in the pursuit of generosity may lead to burnout or neglect of personal well-being. Understanding one's own limits and practicing self-compassion is crucial to maintaining a sustainable and healthy approach to generosity.

Genuine generosity involves giving without expecting reciprocation. However, individuals may sometimes face the challenge of unmet expectations, leading to disappointment or disillusionment. It is essential to approach generosity with an open heart, recognizing that the joy of giving lies in the act itself rather than the anticipation of a specific outcome.

Generosity can manifest differently across cultures, and what is considered generous in one culture may differ in another. Understanding and respecting cultural variations in expressions of generosity is important to avoid misunderstandings and ensure that acts of kindness are received with the intended positive impact.

Cultivating generosity can be as simple as incorporating random acts of kindness into daily life. Small gestures, such as holding the door for someone, offering a compliment, or helping a neighbor, contribute to a culture of generosity. These spontaneous acts not only benefit others but also create a positive and uplifting environment.

Mindful giving involves approaching generosity with intentionality and awareness. Taking the time to reflect on the impact of one's giving, choosing causes aligned with personal values, and being present during acts of generosity enhance the meaningfulness of the experience. Mindful giving encourages a deeper connection to the act itself and the individuals benefiting from it.

Generosity can become a habitual part of daily life by incorporating it into routines. Whether through regular charitable contributions, volunteering commitments, or consistently offering support to friends and family, integrating generosity into daily routines reinforces its importance as a fundamental aspect of one's lifestyle.

Generosity extends to a global scale through philanthropic initiatives and humanitarian efforts. Individuals, corporations, and organizations contribute to addressing global challenges, from poverty and healthcare disparities to environmental sustainability. Global generosity reflects a shared responsibility for the well-being of humanity and the planet.

Technology has revolutionized the landscape of generosity, enabling crowdsourced giving and global fundraising campaigns. Platforms that connect donors with causes, such as crowdfunding websites, allow individuals to contribute to a diverse array of initiatives worldwide. Technology amplifies the reach and impact of generosity, fostering a global community of givers.

Generosity fosters cross-cultural collaborations, bringing together individuals and organizations from diverse backgrounds to address common challenges. Collaborative efforts that transcend geographical boundaries demonstrate the potential of generosity to create a unified global community working towards shared goals.

Ongoing research in neuroscience continues to unveil the intricate mechanisms underlying the psychological benefits of generosity. Further exploration of how different brain regions and neurotransmitters contribute to the emotional and cognitive aspects of generosity may provide deeper insights into its neural foundations.

Longitudinal studies tracking individuals over time can offer a comprehensive understanding of the long-term impact of generosity on well-being. Investigating how sustained acts of kindness contribute to mental health, life satisfaction, and overall quality of life provides valuable insights into the enduring benefits of a generous lifestyle.

Integrating generosity interventions into mental health practices presents an avenue for therapeutic exploration. Incorporating acts of kindness, volunteering, or philanthropy into mental health interventions may offer additional tools for addressing and managing conditions such as depression, anxiety, and stress.

Generosity emerges as a profound force that not only benefits others but also nurtures the psychological well-being of individuals and communities. The joy of giving, enhanced mental health, strengthened social connections, and a sense of purpose collectively contribute to the transformative power of generosity. As individuals, communities, and societies navigate the complexities of the modern world, embracing and cultivating a culture of generosity stands as a timeless and universal path towards a more compassionate, interconnected, and psychologically enriched existence.

Cultural and Societal Influences on Money

Money, a ubiquitous and essential aspect of human civilization, is intricately woven into the fabric of cultural and societal structures. The way individuals perceive, use, and prioritize money is profoundly influenced by the cultural and societal contexts in which they exist. This exploration delves into the multifaceted dimensions of how culture and society shape our relationship with money, impacting financial behaviors, values, and attitudes across the globe.

Cultural narratives play a pivotal role in shaping how individuals view money. Across cultures, diverse belief systems influence the symbolic meaning assigned to money. For some, money may represent success, power, or security, while others may view it as a means to foster communal well-being or spiritual growth. These cultural narratives create a foundation for individuals' financial values and decision-making processes.

The distinction between collectivist and individualistic cultures significantly influences attitudes toward money. In collectivist societies, where communal harmony and interdependence are prioritized, financial decisions often consider the welfare of the group. Contrastingly, individualistic cultures may emphasize personal achievement and autonomy, impacting how individuals approach financial goals and investments.

Cultural rituals and traditions often intersect with financial practices. Celebrations, ceremonies, and rites of passage may involve specific monetary gifts or expenditures.

These practices contribute to the cultural symbolism of money, reinforcing the significance of financial gestures in expressing love, respect, or communal bonds.

Cultural taboos and restrictions can influence money-related behaviors. In certain cultures, discussing finances openly may be considered taboo, leading to discreet financial practices. Cultural norms regarding debt, investment, and wealth accumulation shape individuals' financial decisions and may contribute to disparities in financial literacy across diverse cultural contexts.

The prevailing economic system within a society significantly impacts the distribution of wealth and the perception of financial success. Capitalist societies often emphasize individual wealth accumulation and entrepreneurship, while socialist systems may prioritize wealth distribution and communal well-being. These economic ideologies shape societal norms, influencing notions of fairness, inequality, and the pursuit of economic prosperity.

Societal class structures and the potential for social mobility influence financial aspirations and expectations. In societies with high social mobility, individuals may believe in the possibility of upward economic mobility through education and hard work. Conversely, rigid class structures may perpetuate financial disparities, impacting access to opportunities and shaping financial trajectories.

Societal expectations regarding gender roles contribute to distinct financial dynamics. In many cultures, traditional gender roles influence income distribution, financial responsibilities, and investment decisions. Addressing gender-based financial disparities requires navigating deeply ingrained societal norms and fostering cultural shifts towards more equitable financial practices.

The structure of educational systems within a society plays a crucial role in shaping financial literacy. Societies that prioritize financial education equip individuals with the knowledge and skills needed to navigate complex financial landscapes. Disparities in educational systems may contribute to variations in financial literacy levels and impact long-term financial outcomes.

Cultural definitions of success profoundly influence spending patterns. In some societies, success may be synonymous with material wealth and conspicuous consumption. Cultural norms around achievement and status impact individuals' propensity to engage in consumerism, driving spending behaviors and shaping financial priorities.

Cultural trends and societal preferences contribute to brand affiliation and consumption patterns. The influence of cultural icons, celebrities, and societal expectations can drive individuals to align their spending choices with culturally endorsed preferences. This phenomenon extends to the influence of social media and digital platforms in shaping consumer behavior.

Cultural celebrations and holidays often coincide with peaks in spending. Gift-giving, festive expenditures, and cultural events contribute to increased consumer spending during specific periods. Societal norms around these celebrations influence individuals' expectations and behaviors, creating cultural and economic cycles tied to spending.

Cultural conceptions of status and prestige are often tied to specific symbols, possessions, or lifestyle choices. Individuals may prioritize spending on items perceived as status symbols within their cultural context. The pursuit of these symbols reflects broader societal values and influences financial decisions related to consumption and lifestyle.

Cultural attitudes toward risk profoundly impact individuals' willingness to engage in investment activities. In cultures that prioritize stability and security, risk-averse behaviors may prevail, leading to conservative investment choices. Conversely, cultures that embrace risk-taking may foster a more dynamic investment landscape.

Attitudes toward debt vary across cultures, influenced by cultural norms, religious beliefs, and societal values. In some cultures, debt may be viewed negatively, promoting a preference for financial independence and avoiding borrowing. In contrast, cultures with different perspectives on debt may encourage strategic borrowing as a means to achieve financial goals.

Cultural approaches to savings are diverse, reflecting a range of values and priorities. Cultures that emphasize communal support may prioritize collective savings mechanisms, while others may emphasize individual savings for personal goals. Cultural norms surrounding emergency funds, retirement planning, and intergenerational financial support shape individuals' approaches to saving.

The choice of investment vehicles is often influenced by cultural factors. Cultural preferences for tangible assets, real estate, or specific industries may impact investment portfolios. Additionally, the level of trust in financial institutions, influenced by cultural factors, can shape individuals' preferences for investment avenues.

Cultural and societal attitudes toward financial struggles contribute to the stigma associated with economic hardship. In some cultures, financial difficulties may be viewed as a personal failing, leading individuals to conceal their challenges. Addressing this stigma requires cultural shifts that recognize the broader systemic factors contributing to financial struggles.

The willingness to seek or offer financial assistance is influenced by cultural norms. In some cultures, there may be a strong sense of communal responsibility, leading to a willingness to provide support to friends or family in financial need. In contrast, cultures with individualistic tendencies may place greater emphasis on personal responsibility.

Cultural perspectives on wealth redistribution shape societal attitudes toward taxation, social welfare programs, and economic policies. Societies that prioritize equity and social justice may advocate for policies that address economic disparities, reflecting cultural values that emphasize collective well-being.

Financial values are often transmitted across generations within families and communities. Cultural norms, practices, and attitudes toward money are inherited and shaped by the experiences of previous generations. The transmission of financial values occurs through formal education, familial teachings, and societal expectations, contributing to a continuum of cultural influence on financial behaviors.

Over time, generational shifts may occur in response to changing cultural and societal landscapes. Younger generations often adapt their financial priorities, embracing new values and approaches to money management. These shifts can be influenced by evolving cultural norms, technological advancements, and a desire to address emerging societal challenges.

Cultural expectations regarding intergenerational financial support vary widely. In some cultures, providing financial assistance to younger family members, particularly for education or homeownership, is a common practice. Understanding and navigating these cultural expectations play a significant role in shaping financial decisions within families.

Cultural perspectives on inheritance impact wealth distribution and family dynamics. In some cultures, the passing down of assets is guided by specific cultural traditions and rituals. The cultural significance attached to inheritance influences individuals' attitudes toward legacy planning, estate management, and the intergenerational transfer of wealth.

Globalization has facilitated cultural exchange, leading to a blending of financial practices and values. Exposure to diverse cultural perspectives through media, travel, and digital platforms has influenced individuals' attitudes toward money. Global financial integration has also led to the adoption of international financial practices and investment strategies.

Businesses operating in global markets must navigate cultural nuances to effectively engage with diverse consumer bases. Cultural adaptation in marketing, product development, and financial services becomes crucial for businesses seeking success on a global scale. Understanding cultural influences on financial behaviors is integral to building trust and resonating with diverse audiences.

Globalization has expanded access to a myriad of products and lifestyles, influencing consumer aspirations worldwide. Cultural perceptions of wealth, success, and desirable lifestyles are shaped by global trends, impacting individuals' spending patterns and financial goals. The desire to align with globalized ideals may influence local cultures and contribute to shifts in financial behaviors.

The financial industry faces the challenge of developing culturally sensitive services that cater to diverse populations. Recognizing the impact of cultural nuances on financial decisions is essential for designing inclusive products and services. Financial institutions that prioritize cultural sensitivity can foster trust and better meet the diverse needs of their clients.

Cultural and societal factors contribute to financial inequality. Addressing these disparities requires a nuanced understanding of cultural dynamics that perpetuate economic inequities. Policymakers, businesses, and community leaders can work collaboratively to promote financial inclusion, address systemic biases, and create opportunities for marginalized communities.

Financial education programs must be culturally competent to effectively engage diverse audiences. Recognizing the cultural context in which individuals make financial decisions ensures that educational initiatives are relevant and impactful. Tailoring financial literacy programs to align with cultural values contributes to greater comprehension and application of financial principles.

Facilitating cross-cultural dialogue around money-related topics is essential for fostering understanding and breaking down cultural stereotypes. Open conversations about financial values, practices, and challenges contribute to a more inclusive and empathetic global society. Promoting cultural exchange can enrich perspectives and lead to collaborative solutions to shared financial concerns.

The digital age has accelerated cultural evolution, impacting how individuals perceive and interact with money. Online platforms, digital currencies, and fintech innovations influence financial behaviors and reshape cultural attitudes toward traditional banking and financial practices. Cultural shifts in response to technological advancements will continue to unfold in the future.

Increased societal awareness of the intersection between culture and money has led to advocacy for inclusive financial practices. Movements advocating for fair banking, ethical investments, and culturally sensitive financial policies seek to address systemic issues. Societal pressure and advocacy contribute to shaping financial systems that align with diverse cultural values.

The global challenge of climate change has cultural implications for financial behaviors. Cultures that prioritize environmental stewardship may influence financial decisions, leading to increased demand for sustainable investments and eco-friendly practices. Addressing climate-related financial challenges requires cultural considerations and collaborative efforts on a global scale.

Money, in its essence, is a mirror reflecting the values,

beliefs, and priorities of diverse cultures and societies. The intricate interplay between culture and money is a dynamic force that shapes financial identities, influences economic systems, and contributes to the broader tapestry of human civilization. Understanding the cultural and societal influences on money is not merely an academic pursuit but a crucial step toward fostering empathy, inclusivity, and equitable financial systems.

As we navigate the complexities of a globalized world, embracing cultural diversity in our approach to money becomes paramount. Recognizing that cultural and societal dynamics are integral to financial decision-making opens the door to collaborative solutions, innovative financial services, and a more inclusive global economy. In unraveling the cultural influences on money, we embark on a journey of appreciation, respect, and collective empowerment, laying the foundation for a more harmonious coexistence in the realm of finance.

The Art of Negotiation

Negotiation, a skill deeply woven into the fabric of human interaction, is an art form that transcends cultural, professional, and personal boundaries. Whether brokering international treaties, navigating business deals, or resolving everyday conflicts, the ability to negotiate effectively is a hallmark of success. This exploration delves into the intricacies of the art of negotiation, unraveling its core principles, psychological underpinnings, and strategies that empower individuals to craft mutually beneficial outcomes.

At its core, negotiation is a process of communication aimed at reaching an agreement between parties with conflicting interests or needs. It is a dynamic interaction where individuals seek to reconcile differences, find common ground, and ultimately create value. Negotiation occurs in various contexts, from business and diplomacy to interpersonal relationships and daily decision-making.

The elements that constitute negotiation include interests, positions, alternatives, and concessions. Interests represent the underlying needs and desires of each party, while positions are the specific stances taken during the negotiation. Alternatives refer to the available options if an agreement cannot be reached, and concessions involve the compromises made to facilitate a mutually acceptable outcome.

Successful negotiation is often a collaborative endeavor where parties work together to find solutions that meet their respective needs. It is not a zero-sum game but an opportunity to create value and build relationships. The art of negotiation involves fostering an environment that encourages open communication, active listening, and a shared commitment to reaching a resolution.

The psychology of negotiation delves into the cognitive and emotional aspects that influence decision-making. Individuals bring their beliefs, biases, and emotions to the negotiation table, shaping their responses and preferences. Recognizing and understanding these psychological factors is crucial for navigating the complexities of human interaction in negotiation.

Emotional intelligence, the ability to recognize and manage one's own emotions and understand others', plays a pivotal role in negotiation. Emotionally intelligent negotiators can navigate tense situations, empathize with the perspectives of others, and build rapport. This skill enhances communication and fosters a positive negotiation atmosphere.

Cognitive biases, inherent patterns of thinking that deviate from objective rationality, can impact negotiation outcomes. Common biases such as anchoring, confirmation bias, and overconfidence may lead individuals to make suboptimal decisions. Being aware of these biases allows negotiators to mitigate their effects and make more informed choices.

Developed by Roger Fisher and William Ury in their seminal book "Getting to Yes," principled negotiation emphasizes separating people from the problem, focusing on interests rather than positions, generating options for mutual gain, and insisting on objective criteria for agreements. This approach seeks to create value and build long-term relationships.

Understanding one's BATNA, the best alternative available if a negotiation fails, is a fundamental negotiating strategy. A strong BATNA empowers negotiators by providing leverage and confidence. It serves as a benchmark for evaluating proposed agreements, allowing individuals to make informed decisions during the negotiation process.

The concept of win-win negotiation revolves around creating outcomes that benefit all parties involved. This collaborative approach seeks to maximize value and ensure that each party achieves its goals. Win-win negotiation requires a focus on common interests, effective communication, and a willingness to explore creative solutions that address the needs of all stakeholders.

Negotiations often fall on a spectrum between competitive and cooperative approaches. Competitive negotiation involves a zero-sum mindset, where one party's gain is perceived as the other's loss. Cooperative negotiation, on the other hand, emphasizes collaboration and seeks outcomes that are advantageous for all parties. The balance between competition and cooperation depends on the specific context and goals of the negotiation.

Active listening is a foundational communication skill in negotiation. It involves fully concentrating, understanding, responding, and remembering what is being said. By actively listening, negotiators can gain valuable insights into the interests and concerns of the other party, fostering a deeper understanding and facilitating constructive dialogue.

Clear and articulate verbal communication is essential in conveying messages during negotiation. Nonverbal cues, including body language, facial expressions, and tone of voice, also play a significant role in communication. A mismatch between verbal and nonverbal signals can lead to misunderstandings, highlighting the importance of congruent communication.

Building rapport establishes a foundation of trust and understanding between negotiators. Trust is a critical component of successful negotiations, influencing the willingness of parties to share information, make concessions, and explore collaborative solutions. Establishing a positive relationship contributes to a more productive and cooperative negotiation environment.

Skillful questioning allows negotiators to gather information, uncover interests, and guide the direction of the negotiation. Open-ended questions encourage detailed responses, while clarifying questions seek to deepen understanding. Thoughtful questioning facilitates a more comprehensive exploration of issues and helps uncover potential areas for agreement.

Cultural intelligence, the ability to navigate and understand different cultural contexts, is essential in a globalized world. Cultural differences in communication styles, decision-making processes, and attitudes toward hierarchy can impact negotiation dynamics. Developing cultural intelligence allows negotiators to adapt their approach and build effective cross-cultural relationships.

Being aware of cultural norms and etiquette is crucial when negotiating across diverse cultural backgrounds. Understanding the significance of gestures, greetings, and communication styles helps negotiators avoid unintentional misunderstandings and demonstrates respect for cultural differences. Adapting to cultural norms enhances the overall effectiveness of negotiations.

Different cultures may exhibit distinct negotiation styles. Some cultures value direct and assertive communication, while others prioritize indirect and diplomatic approaches. Understanding these variations helps negotiators tailor their strategies to align with the preferences of the other party. Flexibility in negotiation styles is an asset in cross-cultural interactions.

Patience is a virtue in negotiations, especially in cultures where relationship-building takes precedence over swift decision-making. Investing time in developing relationships can be essential in certain cultural contexts. Cultures that value long-term connections may prioritize trust-building before progressing to substantive negotiations.

Business negotiations often involve complex considerations, including financial terms, contractual agreements, and strategic partnerships. Business negotiators must navigate not only the specifics of the deal but also the broader business relationship. Long-term success in business negotiation requires a deep understanding of industry dynamics, market conditions, and the unique challenges and opportunities facing both parties.

Diplomatic negotiations occur on the international stage and involve complex geopolitical considerations. Diplomats must balance national interests, navigate cultural and historical sensitivities, and work toward solutions that contribute to global stability. Skilful diplomatic negotiation requires a nuanced understanding of political landscapes and a commitment to fostering peaceful resolutions.

Labor negotiations involve bargaining between employers and labor unions to reach agreements on issues such as wages, working conditions, and benefits. These negotiations often carry significant economic implications and can impact the well-being of workers and the competitiveness of businesses. Balancing the interests of both parties is critical in achieving fair and sustainable outcomes.

Negotiation is an integral part of resolving interpersonal conflicts in various settings, from family disputes to community disagreements. Effective conflict resolution requires active listening, empathy, and a collaborative mindset. Negotiators in these contexts often work to uncover the root causes of conflicts and find solutions that restore harmony and build stronger relationships.

Power imbalances can significantly impact the dynamics of a negotiation. Recognizing and addressing power differentials is crucial for ensuring fair and constructive outcomes. Strategies such as focusing on interests, building coalitions, and leveraging alternative options can help level the playing field and create a more equitable negotiation process.

Negotiations may involve individuals with different personalities, communication styles, and approaches to conflict. Dealing with difficult personalities requires a combination of patience, assertiveness, and emotional intelligence. By remaining focused on the issues at hand and maintaining a collaborative mindset, negotiators can navigate challenges posed by strong personalities.

Emotions can run high during negotiations, leading to impulsive reactions and potential breakdowns in communication. Managing emotional responses involves self-awareness, self-regulation, and empathy. Recognizing when emotions are escalating and employing strategies such as taking a break, using active listening, and reframing issues can help maintain a constructive negotiation atmosphere.

Generational differences can impact communication styles, values, and priorities in negotiations. Recognizing and appreciating these differences can enhance understanding and collaboration. Younger negotiators may bring fresh perspectives, while older negotiators may offer experience and wisdom. Bridging generational gaps fosters a more inclusive and effective negotiation environment.

Ethical negotiation involves adhering to principles of fairness, honesty, and integrity throughout the negotiation process. Transparency in communication, a commitment to truthfulness, and a focus on creating mutually beneficial outcomes contribute to the ethical practice of negotiation. Ethical negotiators prioritize long-term relationships and reputation over short-term gains.

Deceptive practices, such as misinformation or hidden agendas, undermine trust and compromise the integrity of negotiations. Ethical negotiators are transparent about their interests, avoid making false promises, and refrain from manipulative tactics. A commitment to open and honest communication builds a foundation of trust essential for successful negotiations.

Ethical negotiators must strike a balance between advocating for their interests and accommodating the needs of the other party. While pursuing one's goals is a legitimate aspect of negotiation, ethical considerations require a willingness to find common ground and seek solutions that benefit all involved. Balancing advocacy and accommodation promotes fairness and collaboration.

Reflection on past negotiations is a valuable tool for continuous learning. Analyzing successes and challenges provides insights into personal strengths and areas for improvement. By identifying patterns, adapting strategies, and refining communication skills, negotiators can enhance their effectiveness over time.

Seeking feedback from peers, mentors, or counterparts is an essential aspect of professional development in negotiation. Constructive feedback offers valuable perspectives on communication styles, negotiation strategies, and areas for growth. Actively seeking feedback demonstrates a commitment to continuous improvement and a willingness to learn from diverse experiences.

Staying informed on current trends, research, and best practices in negotiation is crucial for maintaining a competitive edge. The field of negotiation is dynamic, and new insights and approaches emerge over time. Engaging with relevant literature, attending workshops, and participating in professional development opportunities contribute to ongoing growth and refinement of negotiation skills.

Technology continues to play an increasingly significant role in negotiation. Virtual negotiations, artificial intelligence tools, and data analytics offer new avenues for efficiency and effectiveness. Integrating technology into the negotiation process requires adaptability and an understanding of how digital tools can enhance communication and decision-making.

Global challenges, such as climate change and social inequality, are becoming increasingly prominent considerations in negotiations. Ethical and sustainable practices are gaining importance, and negotiators may need to address environmental and social impact considerations in their decision-making processes. The integration of these factors reflects a broader societal shift toward responsible and conscientious negotiation practices.

In an interconnected world, negotiations often involve diverse participants with varied backgrounds and perspectives. Emphasizing inclusivity and diversity in negotiations promotes richer problem-solving and ensures that a broad range of voices is heard. Future negotiations may place a greater emphasis on creating environments that foster diverse perspectives and contributions.

Complex global challenges, such as public health crises and economic instability, highlight the need for global collaboration. Future negotiations may see an increased emphasis on international cooperation and the development of agreements that address shared challenges. The interconnected nature of the world requires negotiators to navigate intricate geopolitical landscapes and foster collaborative solutions.

The art of negotiation is a dynamic and multifaceted skill that transcends boundaries and empowers individuals to navigate the complexities of human interaction. Whether in the boardroom, on the diplomatic stage, or in everyday life, effective negotiation is rooted in principles of communication, understanding, and collaboration. As the world continues to evolve, the art of negotiation remains a cornerstone of successful decision-making, conflict resolution, and relationship-building. By embracing the principles and strategies outlined in this exploration, individuals can hone their negotiation skills, contribute to positive outcomes, and navigate the intricate dance of negotiation with finesse and integrity.

Financial Education for Children and Teens

In a rapidly evolving and complex financial landscape, the importance of financial education for children and teenagers cannot be overstated. Equipping the younger generation with essential financial knowledge and skills not only empowers them to make informed decisions but also lays the groundwork for a more financially resilient and responsible society. This exploration delves into the significance of financial education for children and teens, the key components of a comprehensive financial education curriculum, and the long-term impact of instilling financial literacy from an early age.

The habits and attitudes individuals develop toward money often originate in childhood. Early exposure to financial concepts and practices sets the stage for responsible financial behaviors later in life. By instilling financial education from a young age, children and teens can develop positive habits, such as budgeting, saving, and investing, that will serve them well into adulthood.

The modern financial landscape is marked by an array of financial products, digital transactions, and investment options. Children and teens need the tools to navigate this complexity. Financial education provides them with a foundational understanding of concepts like budgeting, credit, debt management, and the impact of financial decisions on their future.

Financial independence is a key milestone in adulthood, and early financial education lays the groundwork for achieving it. Understanding the principles of earning, saving, investing, and managing money allows young individuals to approach financial independence with confidence. Moreover, it fosters a sense of responsibility and self-reliance in managing personal finances.

The first step in financial education for children and teens involves introducing basic money concepts. This includes understanding the value of money, differentiating between coins and bills, and grasping the concept of earning and spending. Interactive and age-appropriate activities can make learning about money engaging for young minds.

Teaching children and teens how to budget and save is fundamental to sound financial management. Educating them on setting financial goals, creating a budget, and allocating money for different purposes cultivates a sense of fiscal responsibility. Encouraging regular saving habits, even with small amounts, reinforces the importance of planning for the future.

Familiarizing young individuals with the basics of banking is crucial. This includes understanding how banks operate, the concept of interest, and the different types of accounts available. Introducing them to concepts like earning interest on savings and the responsible use of checking accounts helps build financial awareness.

As teenagers approach adulthood, understanding credit and debt becomes increasingly important. Financial education should cover the basics of credit, the implications of taking on debt, and responsible borrowing. Teaching teens about the importance of maintaining a good credit score and the potential consequences of excessive debt sets the stage for responsible financial behaviors.

While investing may seem like an advanced concept for young individuals, introducing them to basic investing principles can be valuable. Concepts like compounding, risk and return, and diversification can be explained in a simplified manner. Educating teens about the potential benefits and risks of investing fosters a long-term perspective on wealth accumulation.

Financial education goes beyond imparting specific concepts; it should also cultivate critical thinking and decision-making skills. Teaching children and teens how to evaluate financial choices, analyze risks, and make informed decisions prepares them to navigate a variety of financial situations independently.

In an increasingly digital world, digital financial literacy is indispensable. Children and teens should be educated on online banking, digital transactions, and the importance of cybersecurity in financial activities. Building a strong foundation in digital financial literacy ensures that young individuals can engage safely and confidently in the digital economy.

An understanding of basic economic concepts contributes to financial literacy. Introducing concepts like inflation, supply and demand, and the role of government in the economy provides a broader context for financial decision-making. This knowledge helps young individuals comprehend economic forces that can impact their financial well-being.

Schools play a pivotal role in shaping the educational experiences of children and teens. Integrating financial literacy into the school curriculum ensures that all students receive a consistent and structured education in personal finance. This can be achieved through standalone courses, integration into existing subjects, or extracurricular programs focused on financial education.

The effectiveness of financial education in schools relies on qualified educators who are equipped to teach financial concepts effectively. Providing teachers with specialized training in financial literacy and access to quality educational resources enhances the delivery of financial education.

Additionally, schools can leverage external partnerships with financial institutions or organizations dedicated to financial literacy.

Financial education is most effective when it incorporates interactive and experiential learning approaches. Simulations, games, and real-life scenarios allow students to apply financial concepts in practical situations. Interactive learning not only enhances engagement but also reinforces the retention of financial knowledge.

The involvement of parents in their children's financial education is invaluable. Schools can facilitate parental involvement by providing resources, hosting workshops, and encouraging open communication about financial matters at home. Creating a collaborative approach between schools and parents reinforces the importance of financial education in a child's overall development.

Parents serve as primary role models for their children, and modeling positive financial behaviors is a powerful form of financial education. Parents who demonstrate responsible budgeting, saving habits, and wise spending choices impart practical lessons to their children. Observing these behaviors in a home environment reinforces the importance of financial responsibility.

Fostering open communication about finances within the family creates a supportive environment for financial education. Encouraging children to ask questions, express their financial concerns, and participate in family discussions about money helps demystify financial topics. Honest conversations about budgeting, financial goals, and the family's approach to money contribute to a culture of financial transparency.

Providing hands-on learning opportunities is a valuable aspect of financial education at home. Involving children in activities like grocery shopping, creating a budget for a family event, or saving for a specific purchase allows them to apply financial concepts in real-life situations. Practical experiences enhance understanding and reinforce the connection between financial education and everyday life.

Parents can instill a savings mindset in their children by encouraging them to set savings goals. Whether it's saving for a toy, a special outing, or a more significant future expense, the act of saving teaches patience and goal-oriented behavior. Parents can facilitate this process by providing guidance on budgeting allowances and creating a simple savings plan.

Incorporating technology into financial education at home aligns with the digital nature of modern financial transactions. Parents can introduce children to age-appropriate financial apps or online tools that facilitate budgeting, goal tracking, and financial awareness. Using technology in a controlled and educational manner helps children become comfortable with digital financial tools.

Financial education at home should extend beyond practical skills to encompass discussions about money mindsets and values. Parents can share their beliefs about money, discuss family financial priorities, and explore the importance of philanthropy and giving. Addressing the emotional and value-based aspects of money contributes to a well-rounded financial education.

Community organizations and nonprofits play a crucial role in promoting financial literacy. Initiatives led by these entities often include workshops, seminars, and resources aimed at educating children and teens about personal finance. Collaborations between schools, community organizations, and local businesses can create a network of support for comprehensive financial education.

The digital age has given rise to various online platforms dedicated to financial education for children and teens. These platforms often offer interactive lessons, games, and resources designed to make learning about money engaging.

Online financial literacy programs can complement school-based education and provide additional reinforcement for key financial concepts.

Recognizing the societal impact of financial literacy, some governments implement initiatives to promote financial education. These initiatives may include curriculum guidelines for schools, public awareness campaigns, and partnerships with financial institutions to provide resources. Government-led efforts contribute to creating a broader culture of financial literacy within the population.

Financial institutions have a vested interest in promoting financial literacy, and many offer educational programs for children and teens. These initiatives may include educational materials, workshops, and interactive activities designed to teach fundamental financial concepts. Collaborations between financial institutions and schools or community organizations amplify the reach of these programs.

Some schools, especially those in economically disadvantaged areas, may face resource constraints that limit their ability to implement comprehensive financial education programs. Lack of qualified educators and access to educational materials can pose challenges in delivering effective financial education.

The absence of consistent financial education standards across states or countries can lead to discrepancies in the depth and quality of financial education provided. Addressing these variations and establishing standardized benchmarks for financial literacy education can contribute to a more equitable learning experience for all students.

The dynamic nature of the financial landscape, including technological advancements and evolving financial products, poses a challenge to educators and curriculum developers. Keeping financial education content relevant and up-to-date requires continuous adaptation to reflect changes in the financial environment.

The integration of technology provides an opportunity to enhance the delivery of financial education. Interactive apps, online platforms, and gamified learning experiences make financial education more engaging for children and teens. Leveraging technology can bridge gaps in access to resources and accommodate different learning styles.

Collaboration between schools, parents, community organizations, and financial institutions creates a holistic approach to financial education. By combining resources, expertise, and efforts, stakeholders can address challenges more effectively and provide a comprehensive and supportive financial education ecosystem.

Financial education can be integrated into broader efforts for financial inclusion. Programs designed to increase access to banking services, promote savings initiatives, and empower underserved communities financially contribute to a more inclusive and informed society.

Assessing the impact of financial education involves defining clear metrics to evaluate students' knowledge, skills, and behaviors. Assessments may include standardized tests, surveys, and practical exercises that measure the application of financial concepts in real-life scenarios.

Longitudinal studies that track individuals over time provide valuable insights into the long-term impact of financial education. These studies can assess whether individuals who received financial education in their youth demonstrate positive financial behaviors, such as responsible borrowing, savings habits, and investment decisions, as adults.

Gathering feedback from students, parents, and educators through surveys can provide qualitative data on the perceived effectiveness of financial education programs. Understanding the perspectives of those directly involved in financial education helps refine and improve program delivery.

Examining employment and economic outcomes among individuals who received financial education can offer insights into the program's impact on financial well-being. Assessing factors such as employment stability, income levels, and debt management can help measure the broader societal implications of financial education.

Recognizing the global importance of financial literacy, various countries and international organizations have initiated efforts to promote financial education. Collaborative initiatives, sharing of best practices, and the development of global standards contribute to a collective commitment to enhancing financial literacy on a global scale.

Cultural nuances influence the effectiveness of financial education programs. Tailoring content to align with cultural values and norms enhances engagement and relevance. Understanding cultural perspectives on money, savings, and investment provides insights that contribute to the success of financial education initiatives.

In an interconnected world, cross-border financial education becomes increasingly relevant. Globalization has led to shared economic challenges and opportunities. Collaborative efforts to address financial literacy on an international scale contribute to building a more financially literate and interconnected global community. Initiatives that foster cross-border collaboration, such as joint educational programs and information sharing, can contribute to a more comprehensive understanding of financial concepts across diverse cultures and economies.

The rapid evolution of technology continues to shape the way financial education is delivered. Virtual reality, artificial intelligence, and interactive online platforms offer new avenues for engaging and personalized learning experiences. Adapting to these technological advances ensures that financial education remains relevant and accessible in a digitally driven world.

Financial education must evolve to address emerging challenges, such as the rise of cryptocurrencies, changing employment structures, and the gig economy. Including discussions on these topics within financial education programs equips children and teens with the knowledge needed to navigate evolving financial landscapes.

Recognizing that financial knowledge is a lifelong pursuit, there is an increasing emphasis on promoting continuous financial education beyond the school years. Encouraging individuals to engage in ongoing learning, whether through workshops, online courses, or self-directed study, fosters a culture of financial literacy that extends into adulthood.

Financial education for children and teens is an investment in the future prosperity of individuals and society as a whole. By providing young minds with the knowledge, skills, and attitudes needed to navigate the complexities of personal finance, we pave the way for a generation of financially literate and empowered individuals. From basic money concepts to advanced investment principles, a comprehensive financial education equips children and teens with the tools they need to make informed decisions, plan for the future, and contribute to the economic well-being of their communities. The collaborative efforts of schools, parents, communities, and various stakeholders, coupled with the adaptability to technological advancements and global collaboration, are essential in creating a robust financial education ecosystem that prepares the younger generation for a lifetime of financial success and responsibility.

The Role of Gender in
Money Psychology

Money, beyond its tangible nature as a medium of exchange, holds a profound psychological influence on individuals. As we explore the intricate realm of money psychology, it becomes evident that gender plays a significant role in shaping attitudes, behaviors, and beliefs related to finances. The interplay between gender and money psychology is a complex and multifaceted phenomenon, influenced by societal norms, cultural expectations, and individual experiences. This exploration delves into the nuanced ways in which gender influences money psychology, examining disparities in financial decision-making, investment attitudes, and the impact of societal constructs on financial well-being.

Throughout history, societal norms have often assigned distinct roles to men and women, shaping their relationship with money. Traditionally, men were expected to be the primary breadwinners, while women were associated with managing household finances. These historical roles have left a lasting imprint on contemporary money psychology, with individuals often internalizing these expectations.

Societal expectations regarding gender roles can influence financial behaviors. Men may feel pressured to take on the role of financial providers, potentially leading to a greater emphasis on earning, investing, and wealth accumulation. In contrast, women may face expectations related to budgeting, saving, and managing day-to-day expenses, reflecting traditional roles associated with homemaking.

Gendered expectations can impact financial decision-making in various ways. Men may feel compelled to take risks in their financial endeavors to fulfill the provider role, while women may prioritize financial security and stability. Understanding these dynamics is essential in unraveling the complexities of money psychology and addressing potential disparities in financial decision-making.

The gender pay gap remains a significant factor influencing money psychology. On average, women continue to earn less than men for the same work. This wage disparity not only affects immediate financial well-being but also contributes to long-term financial outcomes, including savings, investments, and retirement planning.

Occupational segregation, where certain industries or professions are dominated by one gender, contributes to earning disparities. Women may be more likely to work in sectors with lower wages, limiting their earning potential. The impact of occupational segregation extends beyond income, influencing access to career advancement opportunities and the ability to accumulate wealth.

Negotiation skills play a crucial role in career advancement and salary negotiations. Research suggests that women may face challenges in negotiating salaries and benefits, contributing to the persistence of the gender pay gap. Improving negotiation skills and addressing barriers to effective negotiation can be a key factor in narrowing this gap.

Studies suggest that women, on average, tend to be more risk-averse than men when it comes to financial decision-making. This difference in risk tolerance can influence investment choices, with women leaning towards more conservative options. Understanding these divergent attitudes toward risk is crucial for developing personalized financial strategies.

Gender disparities in investment behavior are evident

in various aspects, including asset allocation, investment style, and risk management. Men may be more inclined to invest in riskier assets, potentially seeking higher returns, while women may prioritize capital preservation and a more cautious approach. Recognizing these patterns is essential for promoting inclusive and tailored financial advice.

Differences in financial confidence and knowledge can contribute to variations in investment behavior. Men may express higher confidence in financial matters, even if their actual knowledge levels are similar to those of women. Addressing confidence disparities and promoting financial education can empower individuals of all genders to make informed investment decisions.

Life transitions, such as marriage and starting a family, can influence money psychology differently for men and women. Women may experience shifts in financial priorities and responsibilities, particularly in the context of caregiving and family planning. Understanding these dynamics is crucial for adapting financial strategies to changing life circumstances.

Divorce can have distinct financial implications for men and women. Women, in particular, may face challenges related to financial independence, especially if they were not the primary earners during the marriage. Empowering individuals, regardless of gender, to navigate financial independence post-divorce is essential for long-term financial well-being.

The role of caregiving, often assumed more by women, can impact retirement planning. Interruptions in career progression due to caregiving responsibilities may affect women's retirement savings and benefits. Recognizing the financial implications of caregiving and developing strategies to mitigate these challenges is crucial for promoting gender equality in retirement outcomes.

Studies indicate that gender disparities exist in financial literacy levels, with women often scoring lower on financial literacy assessments. Addressing these disparities requires targeted financial education initiatives that consider diverse learning styles and preferences. Improving financial literacy empowers individuals to make informed and confident financial decisions.

Implementing educational interventions that cater to the unique needs of both men and women is essential. Customizing financial education programs to address specific challenges, such as the gender pay gap, differing attitudes toward risk, and life transitions, can enhance the relevance and effectiveness of financial literacy initiatives.

Fostering inclusive financial conversations that consider diverse perspectives is crucial for overcoming gender biases in money psychology. Financial advisors and educators can play a pivotal role in creating a supportive and inclusive environment where individuals feel comfortable discussing their financial goals, challenges, and aspirations.

Challenging traditional gender narratives is fundamental to reshaping money psychology. Encouraging individuals to question and challenge societal expectations regarding financial roles can lead to more equitable financial behaviors. Promoting narratives that celebrate diverse financial strengths and perspectives helps break down gender stereotypes.

Achieving gender equality in money psychology requires addressing systemic barriers to equal opportunities and access. Promoting workplace policies that support equal pay, providing mentorship opportunities for women in finance, and fostering a culture of inclusivity contribute to dismantling structural barriers that perpetuate gender-based financial disparities.

Financial advisors play a crucial role in shaping the financial journeys of their clients. Empowering financial advisors with knowledge and tools to recognize and address gender-specific financial considerations is essential. Cultivating a gender-sensitive approach in financial advising contributes to more personalized and effective financial guidance.

The interplay between gender and money psychology is intricate, influenced by historical norms, societal expectations, and individual experiences. Recognizing and understanding these dynamics is crucial for promoting financial equality and empowering individuals of all genders to achieve their financial goals. Addressing gender disparities in earning, investing, financial literacy, and life transitions requires a multifaceted approach that encompasses cultural shifts, educational interventions, and inclusive financial conversations. Breaking down traditional gender stereotypes and promoting equal opportunities in various aspects of life, including career advancement and financial decision-making, is fundamental to fostering a more equitable and inclusive financial landscape.

The Future of Money Psychology

The future of money psychology unfolds against the backdrop of rapid technological advancements, shifting societal norms, and an evolving global economy. The intricate interplay between human psychology and financial decision-making is poised to undergo transformative changes, driven by factors such as digital innovation, changing attitudes toward money, and a growing awareness of the psychological dimensions of financial well-being. In this exploration, we delve into the potential trajectories that the future of money psychology might take, examining key trends, challenges, and opportunities that will shape the way individuals perceive, interact with, and manage their finances in the years to come.

The advent of digital currencies, including cryptocurrencies and central bank digital currencies (CBDCs), is reshaping the landscape of money psychology. As digital transactions become more prevalent, individuals are likely to experience a shift in their perception of money. The decentralization and increased anonymity offered by cryptocurrencies challenge traditional notions of currency, prompting individuals to reevaluate their trust in conventional financial systems.

The shift towards digital transactions has behavioral implications that extend beyond the convenience of online banking. The immediacy and ease of digital transactions may influence spending habits, altering the psychological barriers that once existed with physical cash. Understanding how individuals navigate this transition and the potential impact on impulsive spending and budgeting is crucial for financial educators and policymakers.

Smart contracts, powered by blockchain technology, have the potential to automate various financial processes, from executing transactions to managing investments. The introduction of automated financial decision-making raises questions about the psychological implications of relinquishing control to algorithms. Exploring how individuals perceive and adapt to automated financial tools will be a key aspect of understanding the evolving landscape of money psychology.

The integration of artificial intelligence (AI) in financial services is transforming the way individuals receive financial advice. AI-powered algorithms analyze vast amounts of data to offer personalized financial recommendations. The implications for money psychology involve examining how individuals respond to algorithmic advice, the trust they place in AI systems, and the psychological impact of relinquishing financial decision-making to machine intelligence.

The future is likely to witness the proliferation of tailored financial products designed to meet individual preferences and needs. Personalization in financial services, driven by data analytics and AI, has the potential to enhance customer satisfaction. However, it also raises questions about privacy, informed consent, and the ethical considerations of using personal data to influence financial behaviors.

As AI becomes more integrated into financial services, ensuring ethical considerations in algorithmic decision-making becomes paramount. Addressing biases within AI models, promoting transparency, and safeguarding against discriminatory practices are essential for fostering trust in AI-driven financial solutions. Additionally, leveraging AI for financial inclusion initiatives can help bridge gaps in access to financial services, positively impacting money psychology in underserved communities.

The future of money psychology will inevitably be shaped by global economic shifts, including geopolitical changes, economic recessions, and pandemics. The psychological impact of economic uncertainty on individuals, ranging from heightened financial anxiety to shifts in risk tolerance, will require a nuanced understanding. Financial education and support mechanisms will play a crucial role in helping individuals navigate these uncertainties.

Building financial resilience and fostering adaptive financial behaviors will become central themes in the future. Individuals and communities that can adapt to economic challenges, diversify income sources, and navigate financial setbacks with resilience are likely to experience more positive money psychology outcomes. Educational efforts focused on building financial resilience will be crucial in preparing individuals for an uncertain economic landscape.

The rise of automation, artificial intelligence, and evolving job markets may contribute to increased job insecurity for certain professions. Navigating the psychological impact of job insecurity involves equipping individuals with skills for career adaptability, promoting lifelong learning, and fostering a mindset of resilience in the face of economic disruptions.

The future of money psychology will witness a growing emphasis on sustainable and ethical investing. Environmental, social, and governance (ESG) considerations are becoming integral to investment decisions, reflecting a broader awareness of the impact of financial choices on societal and environmental well-being. Examining how individuals align their investments with ESG principles and the psychological motivations behind sustainable finance will be a key area of exploration.

Impact investing, which aims to generate positive social and environmental outcomes alongside financial returns, offers psychological benefits to investors. The sense of purpose and alignment with personal values can contribute to increased satisfaction and engagement in financial decision-making. Understanding the psychological drivers of impact investing can inform strategies for promoting socially responsible financial behaviors.

Despite the growing interest in ESG investing, challenges persist in assessing and standardizing ESG metrics. The future will likely see efforts to enhance transparency, standardization, and reporting in the ESG space. Addressing these challenges is crucial for ensuring that individuals can make informed and psychologically satisfying choices aligned with their values.

The future of money psychology will witness a paradigm shift in financial education. Interactive and personalized learning experiences, facilitated by advanced technologies such as virtual reality and gamification, will engage individuals more effectively. Customized educational journeys tailored to individual learning styles and preferences will contribute to a more impactful and enduring financial education.

Recognizing that financial landscapes and technologies are continually evolving, the concept of lifelong learning will become integral to financial education. Continuous education initiatives, accessible throughout various life stages, will empower individuals to stay informed about emerging financial trends, adapt to changes, and make informed decisions across different life phases.

The future of financial education will draw extensively from behavioral economics, integrating insights into human behavior to design more effective programs. Understanding behavioral biases, decision-making heuristics, and the psychology of financial decision-making will enable educators to create interventions that resonate with individuals and drive positive financial behaviors.

Virtual economies and the use of virtual currencies within digital ecosystems are likely to reshape perceptions of money. The rise of non-fungible tokens (NFTs), blockchain-based assets, and virtual economies in gaming and virtual reality will introduce new dimensions to money psychology.

Individuals may find themselves navigating diverse forms of value and ownership in digital spaces.

The psychological implications of owning and transacting with digital assets extend beyond traditional financial considerations. Concepts of ownership, value attribution, and the emotional connection to digital possessions will become relevant aspects of money psychology. Understanding how individuals perceive and engage with digital assets will be essential for comprehending the evolving nature of financial behaviors.

The rise of decentralized finance (DeFi) platforms, which leverage blockchain technology to create decentralized and accessible financial services, holds the potential to revolutionize traditional banking systems. Exploring the psychological impact of decentralized financial systems, especially in terms of financial inclusion, will be a crucial aspect of understanding the future of money psychology.

The future of money psychology will see an increased focus on inclusive financial systems, leveraging digital technologies to expand access. Digital financial inclusion initiatives aim to reach underserved populations, providing them with tools for savings, payments, and access to credit. Examining the psychological impact of improved financial access on individuals and communities will be central to assessing the success of these initiatives.

Innovative community-based financial models, facilitated by technology, may emerge to address localized financial needs. Peer-to-peer lending, community investment platforms, and collaborative financial networks offer alternatives to traditional banking. Understanding the psychological dynamics within these community-based financial ecosystems is essential for promoting trust and participation.

Achieving inclusive financial systems requires cultural

sensitivity in the design and delivery of financial services. Recognizing diverse cultural attitudes toward money, financial decision-making, and saving habits will inform the development of financial products and services that resonate with individuals from different cultural backgrounds.

The future of money psychology will witness a more integrated approach to financial and mental well-being. Recognizing the intricate connection between financial stress and mental health, financial institutions, employers, and educational institutions may implement initiatives that address both aspects holistically. Mindful finance practices that promote financial well-being as a component of overall mental health will become more prevalent.

Financial services may incorporate well-being metrics alongside traditional financial metrics. Assessing individuals' stress levels, sense of financial security, and overall life satisfaction can provide a more comprehensive understanding of their financial health. This shift towards a holistic assessment aligns with evolving societal values that prioritize well-being beyond purely monetary considerations.

The recognition of the emotional aspects of money may lead to the emergence of financial therapists and counseling services. These professionals would specialize in addressing the psychological challenges associated with money, helping individuals navigate financial anxieties, conflicts, and behavioral patterns. Integrating financial therapy into broader financial services can contribute to improved well-being outcomes.

The future of money psychology will necessitate a heightened focus on the ethical use of financial technologies. Regulators, policymakers, and industry stakeholders will need to address concerns related to data privacy, algorithmic biases, and consumer protection. Establishing ethical guidelines for the development and deployment of financial technologies will be essential for fostering trust in the financial ecosystem.

As new financial products and services emerge, regulatory frameworks will need to adapt to ensure consumer protection and financial stability. Regulating virtual currencies, decentralized finance platforms, and other innovative financial instruments will require a forward-looking approach that balances innovation with risk management. Striking the right regulatory balance will be crucial for creating a secure and trustworthy financial environment.

Empowering consumers through education on financial products, risks, and their rights will be a central theme in the future of money psychology. Transparent communication, clear disclosure of terms, and accessible information will empower individuals to make informed financial decisions. Financial education initiatives supported by regulatory bodies will play a pivotal role in ensuring that consumers are equipped to navigate the complexities of an evolving financial landscape.

The future of money psychology will be characterized by increased global collaboration in financial services. Cross-border financial products, international payment systems, and collaborative efforts between financial institutions globally will impact individuals' perceptions of financial interconnectedness. Understanding how individuals navigate cross-border financial experiences and the psychological implications of global financial systems will be essential.

Global collaboration will extend to initiatives focused on enhancing financial inclusion on a broader scale. International organizations, governments, and financial institutions may collaborate to address global challenges related to poverty, inequality, and lack of access to financial services. Examining the psychological impact of such collaborative efforts on individuals and communities worldwide will provide insights into the effectiveness of global initiatives.

Cultural sensitivity will be a crucial consideration in

global finance. Recognizing diverse cultural attitudes toward money, financial decision-making, and trust in financial systems will inform global financial strategies. Culturally adapted financial education materials, products, and services will contribute to building trust and facilitating financial inclusion on a global scale.

The future of money psychology is a dynamic and multifaceted landscape shaped by technological innovations, societal shifts, and a growing awareness of the intricate interplay between psychology and finance. As individuals navigate the complexities of digital currencies, AI-powered financial services, and evolving economic realities, understanding the psychological dimensions of financial decision-making becomes increasingly critical.

The integration of digital technologies, personalized learning experiences, and a focus on inclusivity will redefine financial education and empower individuals to make informed choices throughout their lives. Ethical considerations, regulatory frameworks, and a commitment to consumer empowerment will shape the ethical use of financial technologies and contribute to a more trustworthy financial ecosystem.

Moreover, the future of money psychology extends beyond individual experiences to encompass global collaboration, financial inclusion, and cultural sensitivity. As financial systems become more interconnected on a global scale, recognizing diverse cultural attitudes and fostering cross-border financial services will be key to promoting equitable access and understanding.

In navigating this future landscape, the intersection of money and psychology will continue to be a rich area of exploration for researchers, policymakers, educators, and financial professionals. By embracing the opportunities presented by technological advancements, prioritizing financial well-being, and fostering inclusive and ethical practices, we can pave the way for a future where individuals feel empowered, informed, and psychologically resilient in their financial journeys.

Conclusion

I n traversing the intricate landscapes of money psychology, we have embarked on a profound exploration of the human relationship with wealth, financial decisions, and the deeper currents that shape our monetary journey. The chapters unfolded like a roadmap, revealing the complex interplay between emotions, beliefs, and societal constructs that influence the way we think, feel, and act in the realm of finance. As we draw the curtains on this journey, it is fitting to reflect on the key insights and transformative lessons that illuminate the path to financial empowerment.

At the heart of our exploration lies the acknowledgment that money is not merely a transactional tool but a powerful force interwoven with our deepest emotions. Understanding our emotional responses to financial situations, whether driven by fear, desire, or aspirations, allows us to navigate the complex terrain of money with greater insight. Embracing emotional intelligence becomes the compass that guides us through the highs and lows of financial decision-making, fostering a more conscious and empowered relationship with money.

Our money journey often carries the imprints of beliefs ingrained in us from childhood, cultural influences, and societal narratives. Unraveling these limiting beliefs requires a courageous examination of our financial scripts. By challenging preconceived notions about scarcity, abundance, and our own worthiness of financial success, we pave the way for a mindset shift that aligns with our aspirations. The liberation from limiting beliefs becomes the foundation for creating a narrative of abundance and prosperity.

The exploration of cognitive biases revealed the subtle

ways our minds can lead us astray in financial decision-making. Recognizing and mitigating these biases becomes an essential skill for navigating the complexities of investments, spending, and debt. Armed with awareness, we can make more rational and informed choices, freeing ourselves from the shackles of cognitive distortions and embracing a path of financial clarity.

In the pursuit of financial well-being, the crafting of meaningful and informed goals emerged as a guiding star. These goals, rooted in our values and aspirations, provide direction and purpose to our financial journey. Whether striving for financial independence, supporting meaningful causes, or cultivating a sense of security, well-defined goals become the milestones that mark our progress and illuminate the path forward.

The delicate dance between spending and saving invites us to adopt a mindset of mindful consumption. Understanding the motivations behind our spending habits and aligning them with our values allows us to make intentional choices that foster financial resilience. Balancing immediate gratification with long-term financial security becomes an art, and mindfulness becomes the brush that paints a portrait of financial well-being.

The exploration of the psychology of debt revealed the weight that financial obligations can carry on our mental and emotional well-being. Liberation from the bonds of debt is not merely a financial strategy but a psychological journey toward resilience and empowerment. By embracing strategies for debt management, cultivating financial discipline, and fostering a mindset of abundance, we break free from the chains of indebtedness.

The investment landscape, often perceived as a complex terrain, invites us to become informed navigators. By understanding our risk tolerance, recognizing cognitive biases, and adopting a diversified approach, we transform the investment journey into a path of potential growth and financial empowerment. Investing becomes not just a financial endeavor but a psychological journey toward building wealth and securing our financial future.

The intersection of money and relationships underscores the importance of open communication, trust, and shared financial goals. Navigating the complexities of financial partnerships requires empathy, understanding, and a shared vision for the future. By fostering healthy money relationships, we cultivate a support system that strengthens our individual and collective financial well-being.

The pervasive influence of consumerism on our pursuit of happiness calls for a paradigm shift. Cultivating contentment amidst the pressures of materialism involves redefining our notions of success and happiness. By prioritizing experiences, relationships, and sustainable living, we shift from the relentless pursuit of more to an appreciation of "enough."

The transformative power of financial education and literacy emerged as a beacon illuminating the path to empowerment. Armed with knowledge, individuals can make informed decisions, resist financial pitfalls, and navigate the ever-evolving financial landscape. Advocating for accessible and inclusive financial education becomes a collective endeavor toward building a society where financial literacy is a cornerstone of empowerment.

As we stand at the culmination of this exploration, it is evident that the journey of money psychology is not a destination but a continual evolution. It is an ongoing process of self-discovery, learning, and adaptation to the changing landscapes of finance and life. The lessons learned along the way become the building blocks for a future where individuals are not just financially literate but empowered, where money is not a source of stress but a tool for realizing dreams, and where the journey itself becomes a celebration of resilience, growth, and true financial well-being. May this exploration serve as a guide on your own personal journey toward financial empowerment and a richer, more meaningful life.